Praise for
Overcoming Self-Abandonment

"*Overcoming Self-Abandonment* is a must-read guide for every woman who's exhausted by the performance of 'having it all' and ready to finally choose herself. Drs. Hoenig, Smith, and Wilson don't hand out platitudes—they offer a road map back to the most essential, most neglected relationship in a woman's life: the one with herself. With clarity and compassion, they remind us that reclaiming our identity isn't selfish—it's sacred."

—**Eve Rodsky, JD,** author of *Fair Play* and *Find Your Unicorn Space*

"In my clinical practice, countless women come to session and report feeling that they have become everything to everyone—except themselves. *Overcoming Self-Abandonment* speaks directly to that lived experience, acknowledging how selfsilencing, internalized shame, and relational pressures conspire to erode a sense of self. Yet this book does far more than empathize: it offers frameworks and psychoeducational tools to interrupt age-old patterns and nurture a life aligned with women's deepest values. I wholeheartedly recommend it for those who are ready to stop losing themselves in service of others."

—**Jessica Zucker, PhD,** psychologist and author of *Normalize It: Upending the Silence, Stigma, and Shame That Shape Women's Lives* and *I Had a Miscarriage: A Memoir, a Movement*

"*Overcoming Self-Abandonment* names what so many women experience but can't yet articulate—and then walks them home to themselves. Grounded, relatable, and immediately actionable, it's a book I'll be recommending widely to clients, clinicians, and any woman who has ever felt like she vanished inside her roles."

—**Rebecca Howard Eudy, PhD, LMHC,** author of *Parents in Love: A Guide to Great Sex After Kids*

"*Overcoming Self-Abandonment* is a must-read for every woman who is choosing to turn away from the suffocating 'shoulds' in their life and instead choose to live by the words written by Drs. Hoenig, Smith, and

Wilson: 'You are worthy of your time, attention, and care.' This book is an empowering and accessible road map to reclaim the inner work of living your life with clear boundaries and prioritizing your own needs and desires, which is bedrock for thriving in midlife and beyond (or sooner if you are lucky enough to arrive here ahead of most of us). I so appreciated the compassionate and relatable tone of this book and highly recommend it to every woman who is sick and tired of feeling sick and tired."

—**Deb Benfield, MEd, RDN,** author of *Unapologetic Aging: How to Mend and Nourish Your Relationship with Your Body*

"*Overcoming Self-Abandonment* is a practical, grounded guide, rooted in real experience, for women who feel like they regularly lose themselves. Through straightforward advice and relatable stories, it reassures readers that we're not alone and offers concrete steps forward. As a midlife coach and someone who has experienced self-abandonment, I find this book invaluable. I will recommend it to friends and clients without reservation."

—**Sara Smeaton, CPCC**

Overcoming SELF-ABANDONMENT

A Guide for Women Who Are Done Being Everything but Themselves

AVERY HOENIG, PHD

LUCY SMITH, PHD

JAMIE WILSON, PHD

OVERCOMING SELF-ABANDONMENT

Published by
Bridge City Books, an imprint of PESI Publishing, Inc.
3839 White Ave
Eau Claire, WI 54703

Cover and interior design by Emily Dyer
Editing by Roseanne Cheng

ISBN 9781962305525 (print)
ISBN 9781962305532 (ePUB)
ISBN 9781962305549 (ePDF)

Printed in Canada.

The stories and examples shared in this book come from the authors' experiences as licensed psychologists and are offered to help illustrate themes of self-abandonment, personal challenge, and adaptive change. While these stories are inspired by real clinical work, aspects of different individuals have been combined to create the characters you'll meet in the pages ahead. As such, any names and identifying details have been adjusted to fully protect the privacy and confidentiality of the clients with whom we've worked.

This book is intended to inform, inspire, and support—but it is not a substitute for personal therapy or professional mental health care. If you are facing emotional or psychological difficulties, please consider seeking help from a qualified licensed mental health professional who can provide support specific to your situation.

Bridge City Books
An Imprint of PESI Publishing

To our families, friends, and clients who
have inspired us and taught us so much.

Contents

Introduction 1

1. Understanding Self-Abandonment 11

2. The Water We Drink 27

3. How We Abandon Ourselves 53

4. Under the Surface 79

5. Connection and Belonging 105

6. Navigating Self-Abandonment in Relationships 129

7. Upgrade Your Thinking 153

Conclusion: The Essential You 173

Appendix: Feelings List 179

Endnotes 181

Acknowledgments 187

About the Authors 191

Introduction

"You're not the same as you were before. You were much more . . . muchier. You've lost your muchness."

—The Mad Hatter, *Alice in Wonderland*

Emily walked into the therapy office, collapsed onto the couch, and immediately grabbed the box of tissues sitting on the glass side table. She had been at her company for eight years and had been passed over for a promotion once again, this time by a younger man she had hired a few short years ago. Her therapist offered a knowing nod as Emily cried, "I just *can't* work there anymore. I've done *everything* they've asked me to do. I cry in my car during my lunch break because I can't be weak in front of my coworkers. I'm on edge all the time—and it comes out toward my husband and kids. I'm so exhausted by the end of the day I end up just scrolling through Netflix previews, rather than doing something better for myself. I feel like time is passing, and I don't know who I am anymore."

I don't know who I am anymore.

As three psychologists in private practice, we've heard this sentiment echoed by a variety of women. A twenty-four-year-old college graduate aching to find balance in her life, meaning in her work, and a partner she loves while at the same time attempting to please her parents. A stay-at-home mom in her late thirties who's lost herself amid piles of laundry, needy children, and never-ending to-dos. A fifty-year-old empty nester who's struggling to make peace with her body and find peace within herself. A seventy-two-year-old widow attempting to keep her adult children, her partner, and her friends happy while navigating the later stages of life. Although they're at different points in their lives, these women have one thing in common: They've each lost pieces of themselves, and they know it. They *feel* it.

This phenomenon isn't just limited to our clinical practices. We, like you, hear versions of "Who am I now? Where, when, and how do I matter? What about me?" from colleagues, friends, and family members all the time.

The truth is there are three of us writing this book, all established women in our clinical fields, all of us confident, successful and thriving, at least on paper. And yet each of us has had moments where we have struggled to reconcile who we are now and who we used to be.

Avery's Story

My name is Avery Hoenig, and I am a shapeshifter. I spent a large part of my life trying to figure out what people wanted from me and morphing and changing into whatever that was. I'll admit, being a shapeshifter has served me well. Supervisors and teachers have always loved me, I can get along with almost anybody, and I'm really good at keeping the peace. On the other hand, I often get so caught up trying to figure out and tend to the needs of other people that I end up ignoring my own.

When I had a baby, I shapeshifted into the "perfect mom," which I defined as spending as much time with my little one as possible. All while building my own private practice and absorbing all the household tasks.

I was trying to do it all so I could have it all.

I didn't even realize the damage I was doing. Like a death by a thousand cuts, the constant tension between being a good mother who is always available to her child, a good therapist who is always available to her clients, and a good wife who is always available to manage household logistics ultimately made it so that I didn't know who I was anymore. I didn't have the awareness or even the words for "self-abandonment," but my frustration and resentment started to boil over. Taking care of everyone else but myself left me completely burned out.

At one point, I drafted and sent a "contract" to my husband explaining that I was "resigning" from certain household tasks like doing everyone's laundry and cleaning up other people's spaces. The document was my first real attempt to set clear boundaries around my responsibilities at home, but I continued to feel taken advantage of by the unbalanced give-and-take dynamic. It was inevitable that my anger and upset feelings would surface again, and they did. Over and over.

I felt *so* unappreciated and *so* exhausted and *so* resentful, and it was all my husband's fault. Except, obviously, it wasn't.

I had been so outwardly focused on what other people wanted or needed me to be that I had become a master at shifting *all* responsibility outward too. Blaming my husband for everything allowed me to avoid owning up to the part I played in the situation. That is, until he took a sabbatical from work. As he took on the various household and parenting tasks I once held, I had to let go of a lot: My belief that "good" moms or wives should take care of everyone's needs all the time, my own need for control, and my story that "I'm the only one who can do all of this."

Since he has returned to work, I can honestly say we've figured out how to share the responsibilities that go along with managing a household and parenting a teenager. It isn't perfect all the time, sometimes far from it, but working as a team has dialed down my feelings of resentment and given me the time and space to reconnect with the parts of myself that were lost and abandoned over the years. My sense of adventure, my desire for creativity, and my love of writing have returned, and I'm finally finding my way back to "me."

Lucy's Story

"Mom, you're home!" squealed two little voices with delight as they wrapped their tiny arms around my legs. "Will you read us a story?"

I groaned inside, filled with dread and exhaustion. I'd seen nine clients that day and was wishing I'd added a tenth to the schedule simply so I would have arrived home after my girls were asleep. That thought was quickly followed by a wave of guilt. What kind of mom wants to skip out on the bedtime routine with her babies?

I'll tell you what type of mom: the kind of mom who's depleted and burned out. The kind of mom who's been a workaholic and who's forgotten how to truly tend to and care for herself.

I spent years staying busy in productivity mode. I had the capacity to push through for a really long time and jokingly referred to this as being in "industrial snowplow mode," barreling forward while vigorously clearing the ground before me. I was tired all the time, chained to my computer and constantly worried about the next thing. In such a state, my to-dos felt urgent, all-important, and all-consuming. Failure was not an option, not even in the slightest way. Give me a deadline, and I'd meet it with time to spare. This served me well, at least on the surface. I was a "success" by any measure.

And yet I felt utterly dead inside. I was tapped out and frozen emotionally. It's like someone snuffed out the fire inside of me. I felt lifeless.

There was no time or energy for fun or joy. I was tired of listening to others speak, and I'd forgotten how to meaningfully contribute to relationships. I'd lost touch with many of my friends, as well as the desire to socialize. I was surrounded by people and deeply lonely.

I defaulted to life in my head: overthinking, overanalyzing, overplanning, and overcontrolling. I felt lost, swallowed up by everything and everyone else in my life. Where was Lucy Taylor Trenary, the fierce girl I once was?

The gift of being utterly exhausted and depleted is that it creates an opportunity for change. There wasn't a pivotal moment where I had a life-shattering epiphany. Rather, I simply lost steam. I had a growing awareness that I couldn't do this anymore, that I didn't *want* to do this anymore. There was a mismatch between what really mattered to me and where I spent the bulk of my time and energy. I'd lost touch with myself and couldn't *think* my way back. In fact, I felt stuck in my head. To unstick, I had to reconnect with myself and with others. I had to slow down and start feeling. It was truly a process of defrosting.

Things started to change dramatically with embodiment work. By slowing down. Tuning in. Leaning on connection and community. Being vulnerable and allowing myself to be seen. Speaking truth. Showing up as my genuine self.

Jamie's Story

Hello, my name is Jamie Wilson, licensed psychologist and coauthor of this book, and I'm a recovering perfectionist. My perfectionist tendencies began early in childhood and were initially shaped by family expectations, whether that was to keep myself and my room clean and tidy, to fold laundry the "correct" way, or to avoid making mistakes at all costs.

Once I began school, my perfectionism took on a life of its own. I was reserved and quiet, the ultimate rule-follower, and the picture of respect, obedience, and preparedness. Frankly, I was a teacher's dream. I quickly discovered that if I performed well, I would get praise in the form of literal and figurative gold stars, and recognition as the "smart one." The kudos felt great and were quite reinforcing, but looking back, there were huge downsides.

When I went away to college, things didn't come as easily to me as they had before, which was a huge blow to my self-confidence and identity. I was fearful of making mistakes and being vulnerable, especially in a new environment with very limited social support. I struggled. I lost weight and became depressed. I failed classes and lost my academic scholarship. I ended up moving back to my hometown, simultaneously working to pay for school while finishing my undergraduate degree at a local college. I felt immense amounts of shame at that time, worried that I would run into one of my former high school classmates at my job in the photo lab at Kmart and that they would ask with a pitying tone, "What happened to you?"

Until well into my twenties, I would bite my fingernails all the way down to the quick, not even realizing how much anxiety I carried. I was so disconnected from myself that I doubt I could've even recognized and labeled the nail-biting as anxiety. Even after finding my footing and beginning my doctoral training program, I would still hear the constant, nagging voice inside, telling me I didn't measure up and didn't belong in the same league as my peers and friends. I never felt satisfied with my efforts. There was always something more to do, a higher level to be achieved.

I use the word *recovering* to describe my ongoing effort and intention to ditch my perfectionistic tendencies. This has not been easy for me. True satisfaction and joy are never found through perfectionistic striving. Closeness and safety in relationships are never truly felt by pretending to be perfect. I simply cannot be the open, vulnerable, fun-loving, awe-seeking human I want to be by abandoning myself through perfectionism.

My relationship with myself has slowly transformed over time. Through consistent self-compassion practices, many of which you will find in this book, I'm more forgiving of myself. Although my inside critical voice is still there, it's quieter and I don't allow it to run the show.

Our Collective Story

We're willing to bet that if you're reading this book, you can relate to many of the challenges we just shared. For us, and likely for you, too, the

COVID-19 pandemic only magnified those challenges. Each of us felt isolated and overwhelmed, fatigued from providing emotional support across a computer screen all day. One day, the three of us went to brunch and realized we were all in a similar spot: We wanted more creativity and collaboration. We wanted to use a different part of our brains than what was required for our private practices.

We were ready for something more.

We wanted to bring the wisdom and universal truths that arose with our clients to a larger audience. So, we started a podcast, which launched in the spring of 2021, called *Inspiration from the Couch*, and we currently have over 100 episodes. We had so much fun with this project that we started a whole separate business, *The Badass Rebellion*, geared toward helping a wider range of women than those who came to our therapy offices. We've held workshops, book clubs, and various events that have been an exercise in connecting with each other, with our community, and with ourselves.

What we have discovered from this work is that we, as women, are particularly conditioned to follow the script and fit into the mold—to meet everyone else's expectations and be "good girls." We're trained to look outside ourselves to make decisions, to measure our value and worth in terms of our productivity and service to others, and to look to others to validate our own thoughts and feelings. We're taught to be self-sacrificing: to prioritize others' wants and needs and to give up pleasure, rest, and individual purpose.

In other words, we live in a world that encourages us to abandon ourselves.

That's what self-abandonment is: the consistent act of dismissing or suppressing our own needs, wants, desires, emotions, or identities at the cost of our personal well-being, authenticity, and connection.

The pressure to fit in, to be what society deems "acceptable," is palpable and persistent. Over time, we unknowingly give away pieces of ourselves—our time, our talent. We forget about parts of ourselves—our creativity, our goals. We seem to get crowded out of our own lives by our jobs, our partners, our kids. We hustle and overwork. Make no mistake, we achieve great things! However, even amid all this achievement, we end up feeling like it's not enough. We end up feeling like *we're* not enough.

We, as women, are so conditioned to abandon ourselves that we literally change our names to match our roles. Many women take their partner's last name when they get married. Motherhood causes another huge shift in our identities, with yet another name change to "Mom." Of course, transitions symbolize evolution and growth. We are (hopefully!) incredibly proud of these pivotal stages in our lives. But in taking on new names and roles, we also fragment. We lose pieces of ourselves and feel incomplete, which often manifests as the sense that something's missing.

We've also discovered that it's not uncommon for someone to know who they are, what they think and feel, what they want, and what they need—and to be too afraid, too exhausted, or too resentful to speak it aloud. Sometimes, we become so disconnected from ourselves that we don't even know who we are, what we think, or what we want or need.

Whether you have knowingly sacrificed parts of yourself for the sake of your roles or are unaware of the pieces you've left behind, we're going to meet you where you are and help reintroduce you to yourself.

A Few Disclaimers

We'd be remiss if we didn't acknowledge our own privilege. We are three heterosexual, cisgender, white women who have had access to advanced education and lucrative employment opportunities. Inevitably, our personal experiences have impacted our perspectives and worldviews. We aim to step outside of this, to better appreciate and understand the unique experiences and backgrounds of the people with whom we work, and we'll be the first to acknowledge that we might not do that perfectly.

We've made an effort to include a variety of examples and suggestions throughout this book that we hope will resonate with you. You are the expert in you, and we hope that you are able to take the tools that work for you and leave the rest.

Let us be real with you: The work of coming back to yourself is not easy. This book will not make your life "perfect." You are human. There will be discomfort and hard moments. There will be painful realizations as you reconnect to yourself and others. As you're reading, we invite you to approach this book with an open and curious mindset. Give yourself grace and compassion, especially when the work we suggest seems hard. This book is going to give you skills to weather life's storms in a more effective way, a way in which you don't have to continue to abandon yourself, which means that you'll be able to navigate challenges with compassion and connection, instead of with silent suffering and continued resentment.

We've been intentional not to overpromise what you might gain from this book. You don't have to be a marketing expert to understand that sexy sells, as do bold claims, black-and-white promises, and guarantees of *the* solution. We're not here to offer any of those things because, in our experience, they tend not to be real.

Instead, we want you to understand and work with the nuances and gray areas of life. In our practices, we help our clients live with the inconsistencies, messiness, and discrepancies in their lives. We help them identify what they need and determine what actually works for them. That's what we hope to offer you too. So, no, what you're going to read in this book isn't sexy. But we can promise that it is honest and real. We aren't going to recommend any flashy "life hacks" guaranteed to transform your life overnight, but we will provide clear practices and strategies we have successfully used time and time again in our own lives and with our clients. We're not here to sell you anything. We're here to help you listen to and trust *yourself*, not us.

Here's how we are going to guide you in reconnecting with yourself, the self you abandoned, the self that is ready to be rediscovered:

- We'll start by helping you understand what made you abandon yourself in the first place, making space for compassion, understanding, and even forgiveness. Understanding *how* this happened is the key to minimizing self-abandonment in the future.
- We'll give you specific tools to listen to, trust, and prioritize yourself on a consistent basis so you can create more peace and ease in your daily life.
- We'll then take this work into your relationships with others, giving you a foundation to cultivate a strong and supportive community.

You're in the Right Place

If you feel like you're not fully living your life while simultaneously feeling exhausted as if you've been living ten people's lives, or if you feel like there has to be more to your life—more power, more potential—this is the book for you. If you're ready to fully engage in your life and connect deeply with yourself and others, this is the book for you. Instead of abandoning yourself, we'll teach you how to stay connected and tuned in. How to stay present with and for your life.

We know it from our clients and we know it from our own personal experience: *You are worthy of your time, attention, and care.* You have everything you need inside of you; you've had it there all along. As we noted via the *Alice in Wonderland* quote at the start of this book, "You used to be much more . . . muchier."[1] It's time to stop abandoning yourself and to step into connection. It's time to rediscover your "muchness."

Chapter 1

Understanding Self-Abandonment

It's likely that the term *self-abandonment* is new to you. It also might be a bit confusing. You're not alone if you find yourself thinking, *Self-abandonment? How could I possibly abandon MYSELF? Isn't that . . . impossible?!*

We understand. However, we're guessing that while this term may be new to you, the *feeling* may be familiar.

The feelings of resentment, anger, or exhaustion you get when you tend to everyone's wants and needs except for your own? *That's a sign of self-abandonment.*

The feelings of stress, worry, fear, or uncertainty that arise when you don't trust your own knowledge and wisdom and look to others for guidance, opinions, and expertise? In essence, when you don't trust yourself? *That's a sign of self-abandonment.*

The feelings of loneliness, disconnection, or numbness you experience when you're feeling detached from your surroundings or others? *That's a sign of self-abandonment.*

The feelings of distress, frustration, or shame that bubble up when you get caught in a cycle of self-criticism and self-loathing? *That's a sign of self-abandonment.*

The overwhelming pressure you feel to fit into perfectionistic norms? *That's a sign of self-abandonment.*

Take a second to name any of these feelings that resonate with your experience.

These emotions serve as clues that you might be abandoning yourself. But self-abandonment is about far more than how you're feeling in the present moment. See if you relate to Isabel.

Isabel is in her late thirties and has been married for eleven years. She has three children in elementary school. She's always been a high achiever: a straight-A student throughout school, a model employee in her graphic design career before having children, and more recently, a classroom mom extraordinaire who is queen of the Pinterest-worthy party. She ensures her family and home run smoothly and efficiently. Her husband, George, can be helpful in caring for the kids and doing chores around the house when asked directly and specifically, but Isabel is the default parent. She carries all the cognitive load in terms of keeping track of what needs to be done and in executing the majority of childcare and household tasks.

In therapy, Isabel reports feeling frantic, exhausted, and overwhelmed, noting she feels a lot of pressure to do it all and to do it all perfectly. Everything feels like Isabel's responsibility, from ensuring everyone is well-dressed and fed with "healthy" foods to guaranteeing everyone has arrived at all their activities on time and well-prepared to keeping the house clean, organized, and well-decorated. Isabel has a hard time asking for help, both from her husband and from others. She believes she should be able to manage it all on her own, especially since she's not employed outside the home. In addition, she's mindful of the family's tight budget and tends to prioritize spending money on her kids and the essentials. She's reluctant to hire outside help, including babysitters for date nights. Overall, she feels like she can only get help if she *really* needs it, which means she rarely gets assistance or support.

Isabel has a nagging itch that there could be *more* to her life. She'd always imagined she'd be happy with a solid marriage, three kids, and a lovely home, but instead she feels empty, stifled, and uninspired, like she's slogging through the grind every single day. She's incredibly grateful for all that she has, yet she feels like she's missing something. She often describes feeling as if she's "dead ass last"—so focused on getting things done and taking care of everyone else that she has no time or energy left for herself.

Isabel has lost touch with herself. Because she spends her days doing and caring for others, she has very little time to slow down and truly connect with herself. She's so focused on being in "mom" or "wife" mode that "Isabel" mode is a forgotten setting. There's no time for her hobbies or leisure activities, like reading a good book, drawing for fun, journaling about her feelings, or simply sitting on the porch to watch the sunset, all things she'd enjoyed regularly when she was younger. To top it off, Isabel is really hard on herself about all of this. *What's wrong with me? Why am I so burned out, depleted, and irritable?* She feels angry with herself, both for not being content with what she has and also for not doing more to fix whatever the problem is.

The first thing to understand about self-abandonment is that it doesn't happen overnight. Isabel is a good example of that. She has abandoned herself slowly, over time, by ignoring her own wants and needs, sacrificing herself over and over for the sake of others.

Self-abandonment happens consciously and unconsciously. For example, how often do you automatically respond with "I'm fine" when asked how you are? Sure, sometimes you are fine. But sometimes you are *not* fine. Perhaps you've intentionally made the decision to not share how you're really feeling. Alternatively, you might be running on autopilot: so disconnected from yourself that you don't know how you're actually doing.

Like many other phenomena, self-abandonment happens on a continuum. Always responding with "I'm fine" when asked how you are might seem like a small thing, but it's important. *When we get in the habit of abandoning ourselves in small ways, we're more likely to abandon ourselves in large ways.*

Small Ways We Abandon Ourselves	Big Ways We Abandon Ourselves
• Saying we're happy to grab Mexican food when we really want sushi • Automatically saying we're "fine/good/busy" when asked how we are • Pushing through a to-do list when we'd prefer to rest • Sidelining enjoyable self-care activities because they don't feel "necessary"	• Maintaining relationships that are manipulative or damaging to us • Repeatedly numbing ourselves in ways that lead to negative consequences • Staying at a job that makes us feel dead inside • Caretaking others to the point of burnout and personal exhaustion

The Consequences of Self-Abandonment

At some point in life, perhaps even on a daily basis, we all abandon ourselves in one way or another. It's simply not possible to juggle all the roles and responsibilities in life without a great deal of sacrifice and prioritization. Trust us, we get it.

Abandoning ourselves can feel like it *is* working for us. We don't have to think for ourselves when we follow a script. Being productive and meeting high expectations feels great. It feels more comfortable, at least in the short term, to avoid conflict and make others happy, and it feels good to be described as dependable, responsible, caring, and selfless. Aspects of self-abandonment can work for us for a long time! However, inevitably, self-abandonment stops working *for* us and starts working *against* us.

So, how do we know when enough is enough? How can we be certain it's time to reassess, reevaluate, and change?

1. **We feel exhausted.** When we don't attend to our own needs for rest, nourishment, or movement, we feel physically depleted and drained of energy. When we ignore our needs for play and fun, our lives feel uninteresting and repetitive, which makes us even more exhausted. When we don't allow ourselves time and space for connection and meaningful activities that light us up, we feel emotionally spent and burned out. Isabel found herself repeatedly saying, "After this week, things will slow down a bit." She was so busy putting everyone else's wants and needs above her own that she had stopped engaging in activities that were fun and restorative to her.
2. **Our sense of self erodes.** When we abandon ourselves, we leave pieces of ourselves behind like a trail of breadcrumbs. We hope and believe we'll eventually be able to find our way back to ourselves, but over time, we eventually become minor characters in our own lives. Isabel noticed she hardly heard her own name anymore, often answering to "William's mom" or "George's wife" more than anything else. She spent very little time thinking about her own wants, needs, or dreams because she was so focused on others.
3. **Our existence feels "blah."** When we're living in self-abandonment, we're often functioning on autopilot. Just going through the motions day by day. It may feel "easy," but the routine becomes monotonous. We start to dread our days and may feel envious of those with time and space for creativity and adventure. Isabel sometimes daydreamed of running off to a tropical island with no one to ask her what's for dinner and no one to chauffeur around to the endless stream of daily activities. She fantasized about what it would be like to have peace and ease rather than her current feelings of "ugh" and dread.

4. **Our mood changes.** Needs don't respond well to being ignored. When we don't reliably get our needs met, we start to feel irritable, resentful, on edge, and reactive. We can also feel depressed or anxious. At the extreme, we totally shut down and feel dead inside, not really feeling anything at all.

All of this putting ourselves last is really just keeping us on a hamster wheel of busyness and disconnection. We are "doing," but we are not truly experiencing.

Self-abandonment does not just affect us individually. It also has a significant impact on our relationships. It's impossible to genuinely connect with others when we're disconnected from ourselves. And if we show up inauthentically, hiding or shutting down parts and pieces of ourselves, we cannot be truly seen and understood by others. We know from experience that our relationships can get really sticky when our primary focus is meeting the wants and needs of others: We might feel resentful, or the other person might feel like we're too controlling or nagging, both of which ultimately result in conflict.

The Characteristics of Self-Abandonment

In our decades of work in private practice, in our workshops and speaking engagements, in our own lives, and with our friends and family, we've been taking notes and we've identified four overarching characteristics of self-abandonment. See if any of them feel familiar to you.

1. Believing That We Are "Not Enough"

Not-enoughness underlies *all* forms of self-abandonment. This belief that we are somehow not enough—that we don't measure up, that we are less than, that we are worthless—stems from a scarcity mindset. We believe that not only are *we* not enough, but that there is not enough love, success, joy, connection, attention, and so forth available in the world. Sometimes, we are aware of our not-enoughness, and other times, it is a powerful, subconscious force outside our awareness. Not-enoughness often goes hand in hand with self-judgment, and it promotes a hustle-and-grind mentality: *If I do more and achieve more, maybe I can finally feel like I'm enough. Maybe that next accomplishment will finally make me feel worthwhile.* Many systems in our culture (namely, patriarchy and capitalism) leverage not-enoughness to keep us in line and to keep us small.

2. Defaulting to an External Guidance System

When you're trying to figure out how you're feeling about something, do you ever find yourself polling those around you? When trying to make decisions, do you find yourself asking friends, family, or trusted mentors for their thoughts and opinions: *Should I take the new job? Is Larry the right guy for me? Is it safe for my daughter to be dropped off at the mall with friends? Should I cut my hair short or leave it long?* Do you ever consult Google to answer personal questions about your own life: *Should I get a divorce? What makes a good mom? Is this heartburn or hunger?*

As women, we've been conditioned to look outside ourselves for direction and approval. In other words, we've been taught to lean heavily on what we like to call an external guidance system (EGS), where outside feedback trumps our own wisdom, leading us to minimize our own thoughts, beliefs, preferences, wants, or needs. We're taught to make the "right" decisions that will please others. We value others' opinions more than our own.

Similarly, we tap into our EGS when we follow external scripts or expectations: *I guess I'll be a lawyer like everyone else in my family. I really should be married by age thirty. All my friends stop working when they have children, so should I quit my job when I have kids?* Blindly defaulting to scripts or expectations causes our decisions to become divorced from our own internal guidance, which increases the likelihood that we'll make decisions that truly aren't as good of a fit for us.

When we automatically default to our EGS, we send ourselves the message that other people's opinions and beliefs matter more than our own, which leads us to depend on external direction and validation. We ignore our own knowing and intuition, as well as the opportunity to validate ourselves. Other people's opinions, expectations, and rules exist *outside* ourselves, but knowing, intuition, and self-validation are found *inside*. When we forget to balance feedback from others with our own knowing, we're at greater risk of self-abandonment.

3. Ignoring Our Internal Guidance System

Just as each of us has our own EGS, we all have an internal guidance system (IGS) as well. We can think of this as our inner wisdom. Our knowing. Our intuition. As the name implies, the main function of the IGS is to guide, direct, protect, and empower us. It is there so we can be the experts on our own lives.

Unfortunately, many of us don't feel like we *are* experts on ourselves. We trust outside influences instead of trusting our own internal wisdom. We doubt our intuition, believing it's not enough. We spend our days consulting Siri and Alexa, but we've forgotten how to consult ourselves.

While our EGS is loud, our IGS more often speaks in whispers. There's no shortage of outside opinions and feedback about who we should be and how we should live our lives. We're inundated with messages that we can't trust ourselves and our bodies, and we come to believe that, if left to our own devices, we'd languish indefinitely on our couches with an endless supply of potato chips and ice cream. In many ways, society discourages us from trusting ourselves, which leads to continued self-abandonment.

Does this mean that you should throw all external feedback out the window and never ask for advice? Of course not. But many of us have become so disconnected from ourselves that we don't give any credit to our own intuition and wisdom. The work of reconnecting requires us to look inward first, and in the coming pages, you'll discover how to do just that.

4. Hiding From Discomfort

We understand—no one wants to be uncomfortable! We are hardwired to want discomfort to go away, and we spend a lot of time and energy trying not to feel uncomfortable. It's human nature to want to fix things, avoid awkward moments, and run away from anything that will feel hard for us and others.

But we can't. Discomfort is an unavoidable part of being human. Authentically connecting with yourself and others will sometimes be uncomfortable. The good news is that as soon as you give up the notion that you can hide from discomfort, you're freed up to work directly *with* it.

Grieving the Lost Pieces of Yourself

Once you start to recognize that you've succumbed to self-abandonment, you will notice the parts and pieces of yourself that you have lost along the way. When you come back to yourself, you will have to reckon with the choices you've made—both the paths you've taken and the paths left untraveled. This awareness often prompts uncomfortable feelings: regret, loss, grief, sadness, anger, resentment, loneliness, and worry, to name a few. Take heart, dear friend: This is all a normal and expected part of the process. In fact, all these uncomfortable feelings are an essential step in realizing you've abandoned yourself. We often need to experience pain before we can move forward.

Some of you may already have a sense of how you have abandoned yourself and the pieces you've lost along the way. For others, this might still feel unclear. If you find yourself uncertain, befuddled, or disconnected, we have you covered. *The opposite of self-abandonment is connection.* In fact, you can start the process of reconnecting with yourself right now. Simply take a moment to tune in as you relearn how to listen to and trust yourself.

Let's practice.

You can practice this now, or you can block off a separate time in your schedule to tune in. To start, simply slow down and direct your attention inward.

1. Get in a comfortable position, be it seated or standing. Gently close your eyes or shift your gaze downward.
2. Take a few slow, deep breaths to help center yourself.
3. Notice what's coming up in your body right now. What physical sensations do you notice? What emotions are you feeling? What's happening in your head, with your thoughts?

There are no right or wrong answers. Be curious. Be open. Simply notice whatever is happening for you right here, right now.

As you begin the practice of tuning in, you might notice that, like Isabel, you're feeling "dead ass last." Or maybe you have a hard time noticing anything at all. Perhaps you are distracted by your to-dos, worries, or judgments about whether you're doing it "right" or that it's too hard. We could fill the rest of this book with examples of what might have come up for you when you were tuning in. The experience is different for every person, and it is different every time we practice.

As we begin this work, let yourself be right where you are, without any expectation of where you "should" be. Take yourself off the hook from judgment, which we'll discuss in depth later. It's not necessary to beat yourself up for not having known earlier or not having noticed sooner. Many of us have also gotten the message that we "should be grateful and happy," which can cloud our grief and make us feel even worse. We might even start to wonder, *What's wrong with me?*

Spoiler alert: Nothing is wrong with you!

You are exactly where you need to be. You are brave and courageous for showing up here. Trust the process. Trust yourself.

As you move forward, you'll notice some things you want to change, some things you might choose to do differently. You might also feel regret about what you did or didn't do in the past. Unfortunately, none of us can go back in time. When we discover missed opportunities or straight-up losses, we often have to grieve. The good news is when we grieve well—when we really allow ourselves to feel and work through what's coming up for us—we're more likely to reach a place of acceptance and peace. We'll give you the tools to do just that throughout this book.

Maturing Versus Losing Yourself

Maturing is a lifelong process that doesn't happen in isolation. We need feedback from others to help shape who we are and who we will become, and this process of learning, growing, and maturing is a good thing! As we get older, we experience growth by appropriately managing new life roles and learning how to respond effectively to challenging situations. However, self-abandonment occurs when our roles and the hard situations we face swallow us whole, leaving behind crumbs of who we truly are.

Think back to when you were a teen. What sorts of identities did you "try on"? Who and what were your biggest influences? We'll bet you look back fondly at some of your choices and groan and cringe at the thought of others (like the big hair from the late eighties—that was a lot of hairspray!). Most of us have intentionally ditched the hairstyles from our teenage years, but as life shapes our self-concept, we may inadvertently dismiss core pieces of ourselves as well. *That* is where self-abandonment creeps in.

It is important to highlight that both maturity and self-abandonment inevitably involve loss. Unlike self-abandonment, maturity does not mean that you have lost yourself entirely. As you reflect over the life you have lived thus far, we'll bet there are pieces of yourself you've matured out of, such as your tendency to care too much about what others think, your desire to fit in, or your habit of staying in relationships that just don't serve you. These are pieces of yourself that you are probably glad to have left behind because it's led to a more authentic version of you.

If you have a chance, look up the poet Emory Hall and her book of poems, *Made of Rivers*. One beautiful poem in this book illustrates the evolution of a woman's identity over her lifetime.[2] It starts by encouraging you to "Make peace with all the women you once were," goes on to talk about honoring and having compassion for the previous versions of yourself, and ends with "I have been a thousand different women." We love these sentiments.

As suggested by Emory Hall, have compassion for all the pieces of yourself—the ones you can readily access, the ones that feel like a faint memory, the ones that no longer fit, and the ones you've yet to discover. Honor all the versions of you, the "thousand different women" that have led to the *you* that exists today.

So, What Now?

We're willing to bet that you've tried a lot of "self-care" tools to help you feel better about yourself or to feel better in general. We all have! It seems like you can't turn on the TV, flip through a magazine, or scroll through social media without being exposed to wellness-culture marketing, which offers numerous "solutions" to help alleviate stress and "fix" you. Don't get us wrong, true self-care—in which you feel tuned in and connected to yourself—is imperative to your well-being. However, when you get swayed by "self-care hacks" and "coping tools" that are peddled commercially, you might actually end up less connected to what you truly need.

In recent years, we've seen the rise of what's been termed the "joy economy": a $450 billion self-care industry aimed at "helping" people escape the stress of everyday life.[3,4] Many people, especially women, spend hundreds or even thousands of dollars a month on supplements, lotions, and gym memberships. It can be easy to assume that if we're checking off all the self-care boxes in a women's magazine, we are mastering self-care. Ironically, these temporary, surface-level solutions are often marketed in ways that tap into our feelings of not-enoughness—not young enough, not thin enough, not attractive enough—just not enough. Over time, falling prey to these gimmicks leads us to feel like we've abandoned ourselves by a thousand well-intentioned (and expensive) cuts.

Each of us has had clients who go about self-care as if it's another job or task to check off their to-do list. We've also had clients who do *everything* simultaneously in an attempt to increase self-care, which really translates to rushing past difficult feelings. This can look like participating in individual therapy, joining a grief group, volunteering, exercising, reading any self-help book you can get your hands on, watching YouTube videos from "experts," taking tons of supplements—the list goes on. Ultimately, it doesn't matter whether you download a meditation app, get a pedicure, sign up for a pole-dancing class, buy some moisturizer, or go on a vacation. What matters is that you are really tuned in to what you need and that you care for yourself in a compassionate and connected way, rather than frantically, madly, and mindlessly checking another self-care box. Don't worry, we won't provide you with one more external plan you're supposed to blindly follow—in essence, directing you to abandon yourself.

Self-care is important but needs to be done with intention. As you learn more about how to connect with your IGS, you'll get clearer on what you need to do to take care of yourself.

Tuning in and having self-compassion—practices we will reference again and again—will help you find your blind spots, provide clarity, and allow you to truly care for yourself with kindness. At first, you might find it hard to do this solely through self-reflection. You might feel overwhelmed, stuck, or confused. Therapy is a great resource that can help you become unstuck, try out new behaviors in a safe environment, and feel supported as you do this vulnerable work.

We wrap up most episodes of our podcast, *Inspiration from the Couch*, with some suggestions about how our listeners can take the concepts we've discussed and apply them to their own lives. The three of us are proud members of Generation X, and we have fond memories of commercials and TV programs warning us, "Do *not* try this at home." So, we affectionately refer to this portion of our podcast as "*Do* try this at home," and we thought it would be helpful to include something similar at the end of each chapter as well.

Do Try This at Home

#1: Take a Self-Abandonment Quiz

Check any and all that resonate with you:

- ❒ I poll everyone before making decisions in hopes of getting validation that I'm making the right ones.
- ❒ I feel exhausted, burned out, and depleted. I dread my life.
- ❒ I say yes when I really mean no.
- ❒ I'm a pro at avoiding conflict and discomfort.
- ❒ I spend a lot of time in my head, replaying the past or worrying about the future.
- ❒ I have a harsh self-critic. I say things to myself I would never say to a friend.
- ❒ I have a tough time remembering the last time I did something purely for fun.
- ❒ I secretly wish someone else would just take over and make all the decisions for me.
- ❒ I am constantly striving for ways to improve myself, like losing weight, looking younger, or making more money.
- ❒ I have a hard time asking for help.

Generally speaking, the more boxes you check, the greater the likelihood you might be abandoning yourself, though you can still be abandoning yourself even if you only check a few boxes!

#2: Discover Your Lost Pieces

Use these prompts to reflect on the pieces of yourself you might have abandoned along the way. You can simply think about any questions that resonate or use a journal to process and record your growing insight.

1. Where are you now versus where you thought you would be when you were younger?
2. What pieces of yourself from your past have you lost touch with?
3. What regrets, resentments, or frustrations do you need to put words to?
4. What hopes and dreams have you set aside?
5. What are some of the paths you haven't taken?
6. What feels unfinished or unspoken?
7. Which of these can you address moving forward? What losses will you have to grieve?

Chapter 2

The Water We Drink

Imagine being able to *finally* sit down after a long day of doing all the things you do to keep your life going. You turn on the TV and begin flipping through the channels when you see the following commercial:

Ladies, do you want to have it all? Worried it's just not possible? With our handy-dandy guide, Getting Everything You Think You've Always Wanted By Becoming Less of You, *you absolutely can! The perfect marriage, your own home, 2.45 kids, a flashy car, beautiful clothes, a prestigious job, more money—all of this can be yours!*

It's easier than you think. In this indispensable guide, you'll find practical tips and tricks for:

- *Putting everyone else's needs and wants first!*
- *Focusing all your time and energy on looking thin, fit, and young!*
- *Being perfect at all times!*
- *Ignoring your individual hopes and dreams!*

How do you feel after reading these messages in print? Would you knowingly pick up the phone, grab your credit card, and purchase this guide in the hopes of "having it all"?

Absolutely not!

Unfortunately, women have been sold a lie: that we can have it all. That we have infinite choices and freedoms for our career, parenthood, relationship status, money, and fun without very real trade-offs and consequences. You name it, we are told that we can attain *all* of it. However, for women, "having it all" often translates to "*doing* it all."

The notion of work-life balance for women can seem almost laughable at times. Even tremendous professional success does not insulate us from the expectation that home and family life, including caregiving duties, should come first. For example, in an opinion piece in *Newsweek* titled "Taylor Swift Is Not a Good Role Model," the author acknowledged Taylor as a musical and financial powerhouse.[5] However, the male writer's main criticism of the pop icon is that she is unmarried and childless at the age of thirty-four: "While Swift's musical talent and business acumen are certainly admirable, even laudable, we must ask if her personal life choices are ones we want our sisters and daughters to emulate." If Taylor Swift is criticized for her choices on the home front, what hope is there for the rest of us?

It is an interesting and disturbing paradox. We are supposed to prove our worth by becoming partners, mothers, and productive employees, but unlike men, we are also expected to focus on putting the needs of others first while remaining attractive and always being affectionate.[6] We're taught that we should be able to handle all our roles perfectly without disappointing others.

What have you been doing to try to "have it all"? See if you can connect with Maria.

Maria, a twice-divorced fifty-year-old mother, has a nineteen-year-old son who is in his second year of college. She's had a successful career as an attorney and currently works as in-house legal counsel for a computer software company.

Maria is another busy woman. She's uber-productive—a woman who's known to get shit done. She's worked long hours throughout her career: ten- to fourteen-hour workdays are the norm, and when her son was still living at home, these work hours were broken up so she could be as present as possible to parent. For years, she'd set her alarm for 5:30 a.m. and get some emails knocked out before the morning routine, followed by a full day at the office. She would try to leave work by 5 p.m. to pick up her son, feed him dinner, and help with any homework. Then, she would typically log back on to her laptop for a few more hours of work before going to bed.

Maria has some good friends and close family, though her family dynamics can feel complicated and difficult. She often feels like her mom doesn't really listen to or understand her. She was closest to and had the most in common with her father, who died unexpectedly from a stroke five years ago.

Maria doesn't appear to need much from others. She's very independent and self-sufficient. She has spent years saying she doesn't need or want a romantic relationship, but she secretly wishes for someone with whom to share her life. She's filled with self-doubt in response to romantic relationships in her life that haven't worked out. She often wonders, *What's wrong with me that I can't attract the right people?* She has a hard time being vulnerable and fears rejection.

Maria prefers order and logic, thinking and reason. She doesn't really like mushy, messy, and chaotic emotions. No thanks! She often uses her thinking and busyness as a way to outrun or avoid her feelings, and her brain feels overactive as a result—always worrying, planning, and going through her to-do list: *Is my son going to class? Could my mom have some sort of dementia? Do I have enough savings to support myself if I retire in ten years?* Her overthinking serves her well professionally, but she has a hard time shutting it off. She finds herself mindlessly scrolling through social media at night for far too long or falling asleep on the couch with the TV on. She's reluctant to get up and go to bed, as she treasures the quiet time alone with nothing to do—it's her only time off and it helps quiet her busy brain. But she doesn't feel very rested from this "downtime"; rather, she feels more numbed out and disconnected.

On top of all this, Maria has spent much of her life trying to shrink her body down to the "right" size to fit in and belong. Her mom took her to Weight Watchers at age eleven, and in the four decades since then,

Maria has done all the diets and tried every fad. She loses weight with each new diet but inevitably gains it back . . . and then some. She is exhausted from a lifetime of thinking about food and how she needs to change her body. There is a part of her that's starting to wonder whether she'd feel freer if she could stop hating her body and trying to change it. But she is also convinced that everything in her life would be better—that she herself would be better—if she could just lose those extra pounds.

We work with many women who can relate to Maria on multiple levels, who get exactly what she is going through at this stage of her life. But to really understand her and ultimately help her, we first need to understand her context.

It's in the Water

Our lives don't happen in isolation. There are systems in place that impact absolutely everything. Our culture. The environment. Government with its policies, rules, and regulations. Traditions that are passed down from generation to generation. Religion. Our friends. These factors are, metaphorically speaking, in the water we drink each day. It is impossible to not be affected by them. In this section, we will focus on four main factors—patriarchy, diet culture, ageism, and capitalism/consumerism—that set the stage for self-abandonment like Maria's, and maybe yours.

Patriarchy

The word *patriarchy* comes from ancient Greek, meaning "the rule of the father." It is a social system where men have more power, status, and control. In his book *The Gender Knot*, author Allan Johnson writes the following about the patriarchy:[7]

> Patriarchy is a kind of society, and a society is more than a collection of people. As such, "patriarchy" doesn't refer to me or any other man or collection of men, but to a kind of society in which

> men *and* women participate. . . . A society is patriarchal to the degree that it promotes male privilege by being *male dominated, male identified,* and *male centered.* It is also organized around an obsession with control and involves as one of its key aspects the oppression of women. (p. 5)

Put bluntly, patriarchy is a societal system of oppression founded on male supremacy. And if males are supreme, women are, by definition, inferior. Patriarchy is a system of inequality that exists at the expense of women, setting the stage for gender inequality.[8]

So, what does all this mean for women? Through a patriarchal lens, women exist in relation to and in support of men. To take care of them. To have and raise their children. To make a nice home the man can return to at the end of his stressful workday. Inherent in this logic is the belief that women are best suited to domestic endeavors. We're all familiar with the adage "A woman's place is in the home."

For many women, time in the home translates to *unpaid* labor. This holds true for women *with* and *without* paid employment outside the home. Despite significant ongoing progress—with women spending less time on household tasks and men taking on more work inside the home compared to past generations—women continue to carry more of the workload at home.[9, 10] Recent studies suggest that women are responsible for 80 percent of the unpaid tasks required to care for children and to keep a household running, which adds up to an estimated (unpaid) cost of $3.6 trillion dollars per year.[11] Spending more time on unpaid labor reduces the time women have available for other activities, including education, work, and leisure.

A majority of this unpaid labor comes in the form of an invisible cognitive load,[12] which can be likened to a full-time job of "household manager" that runs twenty-four hours a day, seven days a week. This job requires that you always identify what needs to be done, plan how it'll get accomplished, and keep track to ensure it happens. If you recall

Isabel from the previous chapter, she is the default parent when it comes to her kids. And since all her children play sports, that means she is responsible for keeping up with the emails and messaging apps regarding her children's practice, game-day, and snack schedules. She's in charge of ordering uniforms and ensuring each child shows up with the correct gear, as well as figuring out the schedule for who will take each child where. When her husband helps, it is because he has been assigned specific tasks that he can accept or decline, while Isabel is the mastermind behind and is responsible for the whole system.

The invisible cognitive load does not only apply to little league sports. It includes *everything*. No wonder we women are so exhausted!

Remember, that's just the unpaid labor. When it comes to paid labor, large discrepancies in earnings for women abound. Approximately one-third of workers in the ten highest-paying industries in the United States are women, and across all industries, women get paid less for doing the same work as men. For example, in 2022, women earned eighty-two cents to every dollar earned by a man, which was up only two cents from 2002.[13] This amounts to a $172 billion earning difference between men and women over the course of their lifetimes.[14]

Women are also impacted financially because they tend to have more interruptions to their careers. Women often take more time off from work to care for their family, be it raising their own children or tending to aging parents.[15] Not only does this further reduce their savings, but it also disrupts the trajectory of their career. In fact, some women choose to leave the workforce or take on lower-paying jobs to have more flexibility and time for their families.[16] While most industries grant maternity leave as a norm, paternity leave is rarely offered.[17] The message we receive is that Mom is expected to stay home with the baby and Dad is expected to go back to work.

Women are treated differently than men in the workplace as well, which makes for a less hospitable environment. While sex discrimination is illegal in the workplace, women are regularly passed over for promotions, not supported by senior leadership, and sidelined once they become pregnant or have kids. Women also typically hold fewer seats in government and are underrepresented in leadership positions across corporations.[18]

However, women don't just endure bias and discrimination inside the workplace—they do outside of it as well. For example, women are often not treated with respect when engaging in traditionally male activities like financial matters, home repairs, and car maintenance. Women pay more to own a car in both purchase price and repairs,[19, 20] and doctors are more likely to gaslight female patients about their physical and mental health, minimizing, dismissing, or misdiagnosing their symptoms.[21, 22] Let's also not forget how women are constantly seen as objects of desire who exist for men's pleasure. Women endure unwanted attention constantly. Physical, emotional, and sexual abuse are both a manifestation and consequence of a patriarchal mindset, and while we have made strides, this reality still exists.

Finally, under the system of patriarchy, women have fewer opportunities, as well as restricted freedom, autonomy, and independence. It has only been in recent decades that women have had equal access to education. For centuries, women couldn't vote, make their own money, own property in their name, open a bank account, or choose whom they wanted to marry. Women were not allowed to be autonomous or independent until very recently. Sadly, this lack of control and decision-making continues for many women in the world today.

Although men have privilege in this system, *everyone* suffers under the patriarchy. Women suffer. People who identify as non-heterosexual or gender nonconforming suffer. Men suffer, as the patriarchy only makes space for masculine aspects of the self, such as not showing emotions other than anger and always being a "strong" and dominating provider.[23]

If women are viewed as inferior to and existing only in relation to and in support of men, how could we not abandon ourselves? *A patriarchal system both requires and rewards women for abandoning themselves.* Even with progress toward equality, the lingering and underlying system of oppression makes it hard to stay truly connected to ourselves. It is no wonder that so many of us lose pieces of ourselves and abandon our hopes and dreams.

Diet Culture

Diet culture is prevalent, pervasive, and costly: Approximately forty-five million Americans diet every year, and we spend over seventy billion dollars a year on the diet industry.[24, 25] However, we have 100 years of research showing that diets don't work[26] and, thankfully, there's growing awareness that people don't fail their diets—the diet industry fails them. It's not that *we* are doing it wrong or that *we* are weak or don't have willpower, discipline, or motivation. *It's that diets don't work.* Period.

While diets aren't typically successful in helping people lose weight over the long term, the diet industry continues to be lucrative because it preys upon our not-enoughness. Diet culture tells us that thinner is better and that thinner bodies (and, by extension, thinner people) are more valuable. While much of diet culture has rebranded itself to talk more about "health" and "wellness," it's ultimately still about losing weight and being thin. "Health" trends dictate when, how, and what to eat, while "wellness" trends encourage us to exercise to burn calories, tone our bodies, and get fit and strong. The more we move our bodies, the better. In essence, diet culture keeps us trapped by promising that if we eat the "right" things and move our bodies the "right" way, we'll lose weight, be thin, and *finally* feel like we're enough.

We live in a world where people are constantly judged for their body size and shape, with particularly harsh judgment against people in larger bodies. There is so much shame and blame associated with body size, including the belief that being in a larger body is a moral failing and a preventable choice. Weight stigma is especially harmful because it often occurs in our most trusted relationships. Under the guise of wanting to "help" us be "healthy," uninformed family members, friends, and health professionals may say incredibly hurtful things about our bodies as an act of "tough love." Commentary about our bodies and eating choices is *never* helpful, whether it's unsolicited advice about what we should be eating, comments on how we should be moving our bodies, or a doctor's firm insistence that we need to drop a few pounds.

It's no wonder we place so much pressure on ourselves and spend so much time and money to be thin. It's also no wonder that our efforts so often backfire. Rather than delivering enoughness, we experience negative consequences as a result of diet culture, such as body dissatisfaction, mental health struggles (stress, anxiety, depression), disordered eating or full-blown eating disorders, and a preoccupation with eating, weight, and shape.

Of course, we sacrifice so much more than just time and money to diet culture. The problem is so much bigger than that. Many of us devote an inordinate amount of attention and emotional energy trying to whip our bodies into shape because diet culture is rooted in the belief that we can't trust ourselves or our bodies. We must instead control and manage them. Our preoccupation with our bodies, the power we give to being thin, and our tendency to put our lives on hold until we lose weight all keep us trapped in dieting. We believe that once we are whipped into shape, everything else will magically fall into place—we'll be happy and our lives will be perfect. Diet culture is a large external system that ultimately needs to be dismantled, and little acts of rebellion (like refusing to let the system dictate how you choose to live your life) can go a long way.

As with the other systems at play, there is growing awareness about sizeism (i.e., discrimination based on a person's size or weight) and diet culture. In turn, specific movements have evolved to counter diet culture and weight stigma. This includes the anti-diet movement, the body positivity movement, weight-neutral fitness, and the Health at Every Size (HAES)® approach. There is also a growing awareness of "fat shaming," as we regularly hear teens and young adults making comments like "Don't fat shame me" or "Yuck, that's so much diet culture talk." This younger generation is several steps ahead in their ability to recognize and name these systemic forces. While we are all still impacted by the pernicious messaging of diet culture, by naming it, we can intentionally work with and better disconnect from it.

At the end of the day, diet culture can make us believe that being thin makes us more lovable and more worthy, and who wouldn't want to chase that? Most of us would do anything to feel worthy and enough. But the system is a setup from the beginning. Our enoughness comes from inside. Our body shape and size have nothing to do with our lovability or worth. When we shrink ourselves down to fit into an external standard, we're likely to abandon ourselves in the process. Take a moment to consider how much precious time and energy you have spent trying to make your body fit into what society deems acceptable. How much of yourself has been lost along the way? Instead of changing or controlling your body to fit into the diet culture standard, could you change the relationship you have with diet culture? What could happen if you were able to truly accept and value your body, no matter its shape or size? Could you treat your body with kindness and compassion rather than constantly trying to whip it into shape?

We get it, breaking up with diets can sound like an impossible feat. But we've also seen the impossible become possible when individuals base their worth and value on who they are on the *inside* rather than the *outside*.

Ageism

For many of us, aging feels scary and undesirable. After all, we are inundated with messages that we need to look young and attractive if we want to be taken seriously in the world as women. Society pressures us to look as young as possible for as long as possible, and it's not uncommon to feel less desirable, less attractive, and even less significant as we age. The global anti-aging market is yet another multibillion-dollar business fueled by not-enoughness. This market was valued at $63 billion in 2021 and is projected to reach $93 billion by 2027.[27]

The workplace is a breeding ground for age-based discrimination, particularly for women. For example, a recent study on ageism in the workplace found that women of *all* ages are impacted by the "never-right" age bias, which is the phenomenon where women are never viewed as being the "right" age for leadership in the workplace, no matter how old they are.[28] In particular, younger women are talked down to and not believed to be credible. Older women are seen as dried up, washed out, and not worth investing in. Middle-aged women are seen as having too many family obligations and being emotionally unstable due to the likelihood of entering menopause. As you can see, there is no "right" age for women in the workplace! We're beginning to wonder if there's a "right" age for women any place!

Let's be real: Most of us have some tips and tricks that help us look and feel youthful—from highlighting our hair to splurging on our favorite anti-aging skin creams. We're not here to judge, and we're not here to police investments in time, money, and energy that feel good and right to you. But we are here to invite you to be curious about the motivation behind and the outcomes of these efforts. In other words, are these investments a way to stay connected to yourself and genuinely care for yourself? Or are these investments another form of self-abandonment, a way to disconnect from yourself and the present?

Ageism leads to self-abandonment when we buy into the message that who we are, at whatever age, is not okay. We abandon ourselves when we become obsessed with our outward appearance and go to drastic lengths to try to change ourselves so we can fit into a system that prioritizes young, pretty, and thin women.

In contrast, when we stay connected to ourselves, we make space for the entire experience: a sense of loss as our bodies and minds age and slow down, but also a sense of clarity around what matters most. When we reconnect with our true selves, we can find joy in the present, connect with the world around us, and celebrate the wisdom that we've earned over the years.

Capitalism and Consumerism

Capitalism equates our worth with what we produce. When we feel like we're not enough, we do more and consume more to try to compensate for this perceived inadequacy, and capitalism thrives. This plays out clearly with our appearance: We have to be attractive, thin, and young-looking to fit in, and because we clearly fall short of all these ideals on our own, we need to spend a lot of money—to invest in products and services—to help us.

This sets us up for a no-win feedback loop. When we are driven by the belief that more stuff, products, and "solutions" will make us happier, we externally focus on consuming. We spend our hard-earned money, experience a temporary increase in happiness, and ultimately return to discontent and not-enoughness. We work more so we can earn more, and then we spend more on solutions, which again lead to temporary happiness, followed by longer-lasting not-enoughness. It's never-ending.

When we focus on things outside of ourselves, particularly on spending and consuming, it interferes with our ability to truly connect to ourselves and others. We instead spend a lot of time accumulating, which takes away from aspects of our lives that are really rewarding and meaningful. In his book *The High Price of Materialism*, Tim Kasser describes research showing that people who organize their lives around extrinsic goals, such as product acquisition, report greater unhappiness in relationships, poorer moods, and more psychological problems.[29] He makes the point that it's the constant *aspiration* to have more things or achieve greater wealth that is associated with more unhappiness. It's a bidirectional relationship—when we're unhappy, we tend to consume more, and consuming more leads to unhappiness!

We All Drink the Water

The dynamics from these four systems are deeply rooted in our culture. In our research, we've found that acknowledging these forces is the first step in reclaiming yourself. These systems are not something you've "fallen for" or something you're "guilty of." It's not your fault! These are insidious systems that have operated below your consciousness for years. We've all been impacted by them. We've internalized their messages. Yes, it would be amazing if these systems themselves were changed or ceased to exist. We will have to keep working on that collectively. But in the meantime, each of us can become more aware of the proverbial water we drink and can start to challenge the "truths" we've been told.

Self-Abandonment Versus Self-Preservation

Before moving on, we want to differentiate self-abandonment behaviors (that we can and should identify and change) from survival behaviors that are more about preservation of safety and livelihood. For example, consider a woman who really wants to watch her favorite movie on TV, but her husband insists on watching the football game. She knows she'll be berated for even asking if they can change the channel, so she plays along and pretends to enjoy the college game-day programming. Or consider another woman who meticulously covers her gray roots, maintains a slim physique, and shows no emotions so she can keep her executive leadership role (as she's watched many women before her be fired when they show signs of aging or vulnerability).

In some ways, as we've defined it, these women are "abandoning" themselves by not speaking truth and by hiding parts of themselves. However, these situations feel very different from self-abandonment. For starters, in these examples, the women acknowledge who they are and what they really want and need, and this genuine connection to themselves is the exact opposite of self-abandonment. Although they are—in varied ways—following a script or putting on a mask, this is more about protection, self-preservation, and survival.

Patriarchy. Diet culture. Ageism. Capitalism and consumerism. These are the systems at play in our culture. Although these systems are *outside* us, we often *internalize* their messages. We do this by being the good girl, hustling, and seeking the perfect, curated life. Now, let's talk about how these systems shape how we show up in the world.

Good-Girl Mentality

Maria, who we met at the beginning of this chapter, described herself as being a "good little girl" in childhood. She did her schoolwork, listened to the teacher, and stayed quiet during class. She was often rewarded for her good behavior by being seated between the "rowdy" boys who could not keep their voices down or their hands to themselves. Throughout school, she got the message loud and clear: Her job was to follow the rules and not take up too much space, literally and figuratively.

Maria got married just shy of her twenty-sixth birthday. She worked tirelessly to balance her new household responsibilities with her demanding first-year associate position. She was able to take maternity leave after her son was born and dutifully denied herself basic needs, like eating regularly and getting enough sleep and movement, to be a "good mom" and prioritize caring for her infant. When she returned to work, Maria did what she thought she was supposed to do and never asked for help.

She was exhausted all the time, never had time for herself, and began to see her husband more as a roommate than a partner. She rarely caught up with her friends, and when she did, she didn't feel like she could be honest about her struggles. She felt unbelievably lonely, but she kept her head down and just kept on marching forward. By the time her son started kindergarten, she hardly felt like she knew her husband (or herself) anymore. She never thought that she would be the kind of person to get a divorce, but her marriage fell apart nonetheless.

The good-girl identity is based on the dichotomous belief that you must follow the good-girl script perfectly or risk losing your good-girl status entirely. There is no room for mistakes. Any misstep and you are deemed a bad girl or any of the other terrible names we use to refer to women who aren't following the rules.

Of course, following the rules is a direct route to abandoning yourself. See if you can identify which of these good-girl rules you have internalized:

- **Good girls are chaste.** Shame and guilt keep good girls in line like bumpers in a bowling alley. Desire is shameful and pleasures are guilty, so good girls learn to silence their desires and abstain from pleasure. Good-girl morality often has a religious and patriarchal undertone to it as well: You must remain "pure" and "save" yourself for marriage. Experiencing or acting on sexual desires makes you a "bad" girl or any number of negative sexual slurs used to describe women. *Translation: Desire and pleasure are dangerous.*
- **Good girls are polite.** Good girls learn to prioritize being nice over being honest. Good girls don't want to cause problems or be difficult. Women who speak up and voice their opinions are often dismissed as bossy, bitchy, and unladylike. Good girls keep their mouths shut. Rather than identifying their own truth and speaking it honestly and authentically, good girls choose a well-mannered response to any situation. They want to be agreeable, so they ignore their IGS, especially if it goes against the "way things have always been done." *Translation: Girls are only "good" when they keep the status quo.*
- **Good girls are only allowed to feel happy, content, and grateful.** Good girls learn that some feelings, like anger, should be suppressed and kept inside. In turn, they learn to mask their negative feelings and carry this lesson into adulthood. Not wanting to complain or seem ungrateful, they don't discuss the difficult emotions that go along with certain life experiences, like the first year of marriage, the newborn stage of parenthood, or the constant push and pull of balancing work and family. Instead, they push the

uncomfortable feelings away, further disconnecting from others and abandoning themselves. *Translation: Never express any negative emotion, under any circumstance.*

- **Good girls are always available to everyone all the time.** They're programmed to not wander too far outside of their roles (daughter, friend, wife, mother, coworker) and learn that having needs of their own makes them "needy." Not wanting to seem demanding or "high maintenance," good girls keep their wants and needs to themselves. They focus their time, effort, and energy on meeting the needs of others, eventually becoming crowded out of their own lives. *Translation: A good girl's needs come last.*

To be clear, being a good girl is not all bad. It feels good to get the "atta girl" kudos that comes with following the rules and fulfilling our roles. It's uncomfortable to cause conflict and go against the grain, so we're tempted to play it safe and not venture outside of our comfort zones. There can be a sense of pride, meaning, and worth that comes from being good at taking care of the people in our lives. All this positive feedback makes it hard to put down the good-girl identity.

However, when we are focused on following external rules, we bypass our intuition and internal wisdom. We default to an EGS and ignore our IGS. We sacrifice parts of ourselves and abandon ourselves. For example, Maria acted the part of "good girl," "good wife," and "good mom," but following the rules didn't leave space for her to show up in her life as she really was. She couldn't stay connected to herself or the people around her because she didn't feel allowed to show her real, flawed, human self. It is in this way that the good-girl mentality often causes more harm than good.

Uber-Productivity and Hustle Culture

When you're asked how you're doing, how often do you reply "BUSY!"? Busyness has become our default, and for those of us who know the value of being honest with our feelings, this is a big problem. It's not that we are deliberately trying to stay busy to avoid sharing who we are and what's going on for us. We *are* busy! The problem is that we're all so damn busy we can't really see or feel anything except for this busyness. "Busy" has become a status symbol, a dubious badge of honor.

Society conditions us to be productive, to multitask, to handle everything at the same time. In other words, it is not enough to get things done. We must be uber-productive by doing anything and everything all the time. Hustle culture asks us to overwork and constantly push ourselves harder, all for the promise of future "success." Often, the vague definition of success tends to include more money, a big break, a promotion, securing the dream job, a chiseled body, status, and renown. Unfortunately, with hustle culture, there is never an end point—there's always more work to be done, another goal to chase.

You can imagine how living this way can erode our sense of who we are and what we truly value.

We've come to entangle our identity and worth with how much we do and what we achieve. In essence, we have become human *doings* instead of human *beings*. When we are so fixated on our to-do lists, there's not much space or bandwidth to rest or to connect. We run ourselves ragged, and most of us are utterly exhausted. We are burned out, yet being still can make us feel anxious and unsettled. We are quite literally restless and disconnected from our bodies. We are terrified to slow down or do less—we fear losing our jobs, losing our edge, being outperformed, and feeling not enough or less than.

Hustle culture thrives on comparison and competition. We are driven by the need to be *better than*—better than others, better than our past performance, better than expectations and ideals. Every workout needs to be a personal record. Every snack should be healthier and more visually appealing than the last. Every performance review must exceed expectations.

We feel immense judgment, guilt, and shame when we're not being productive. For example, in one therapy session, Maria was sharing about her day, and she sheepishly described how "lazy" she'd been. She said, "I planned to be super productive, but I had a cancellation in my schedule, so I ended up going to get a pedicure, followed by dinner and live music with friends." She was almost apologetic about "wasting" her time, and she clearly felt guilty and conflicted about having set her to-do list aside. Where in the world did we get the idea that making appointments and reorganizing our offices are a more valuable use of our time than taking care of ourselves and connecting with others? Yes, mammograms need to be scheduled and spaces need to be decluttered, but why are those tasks *more* important than leisure endeavors?

If we are so exhausted and depleted, why do we continue to overwork and over-hustle? First, we get lots of proverbial gold stars for working hard and being productive. We are reinforced by society with praise for our ability to accomplish so much. Our work culture often rewards long hours, particularly in high-pressure fields, with more money, promotions, titles, and, ironically, more work. Not only that, but many of us overwork to distract or numb, to fill the void of not-enoughness, to avoid relationships and connection, and to avoid uncomfortable feelings. Uber-productivity serves a powerful purpose.

Let us be clear: It's not bad to be productive or to work hard. Hustle is exciting and appropriate from time to time. The problem arises when we *over*do it. We suffer when we chronically prioritize productivity and to-dos over connection and presence.

Bottom line: The system is a cycle that continues in perpetuity. We feel like we are not enough, so we work harder and push ourselves even more, yet we *still* don't feel like we're enough, making us double down on the hustle. When we get too focused on achieving, checking off our to-do lists, or being productive, we miss so many important things: connection, friendships, leisure, fun, joy, and pleasure. We de-prioritize the good stuff in life, instead letting work and tasks take center stage over relationships and presence. We can become lonely and feel like a shell of our former selves. Ultimately, we sacrifice ourselves in the process, and self-abandonment is the inevitable consequence.

A Curated Existence

Isabel and her kids had plans to meet new friends from school for a playdate, but she got a sinking feeling in the pit of her stomach as soon as she pulled into the driveway. The house was huge, gorgeous, and perfectly landscaped. *We'll never be able to have these people over—our home is tiny compared to this mansion,* she thought.

As she got her kids out of the car, she caught a reflection of herself in the window. She rolled her eyes and muttered under her breath, "How could I go out like this? I look like shit!" She was frantically trying to comb through her hair with her fingers and straighten her shirt when her new mom friend came to the door. Isabel coveted her effortless style and made a mental note, *I've got to do some online shopping when I get home.*

The kids got along great and the fashionable mom was incredibly kind, but Isabel left feeling awful. Not only had she spent the past two hours beating herself up for her various shortcomings, but she had also become so fixated on what she could do to improve her home, her outfit, and herself that she had a hard time being present and connecting with her new friend.

Many of us have a similar experience when we feel like we are not measuring up. When we are preoccupied with how we present to the outside world, we struggle to stay present in the moment. If we believe that when everything looks right, everything will be all right, we get hung up on things that don't actually matter. We get obsessed with acquiring the right outfit or the right house or whatever "looks right" in the hopes that we'll "be all right"—that we'll finally fit in and have worth and value. These "right" things become a proxy for enoughness, but they don't deliver what we're seeking. The "right" things do not help us stay connected with ourselves or others. In fact, we actually *lose* connection in the pursuit of them.

In other words, chasing a curated existence keeps us focused on obtaining the next "right" thing, leaving little room for us to tune in to ourselves or show up authentically in our relationships.

As we've already talked about, modern day society makes coming back to ourselves easier said than done. Social media has become a primary source of information and feedback; it's the first place we often look to figure out who we need to be. However, both what we share and see on social media are not fully authentic. Most people show up on social media in a surface-level, unidimensional way, only showing select parts of their lives. They create a highlight reel of their days and project a filtered version of themselves—an avatar with a curated life. Most of us end up comparing our insides, which tend to be messy, to other people's outsides, which are presented perfectly. Ultimately, we end up feeling bad about ourselves and come away with an inaccurate sense of what's normal.

This can, of course, translate to our relationships in real life. We hide our perceived imperfections and present inauthentic versions of ourselves to one another. We don't show up in our lives as our true selves, faults and all. All this means that genuine connection with others is practically impossible.

We've all had the experience of trying to keep up with the Joneses (or Kardashians) in one way or another, but when we use someone else's template for a "good life," we pursue things that ultimately do not bring us authentic meaning and joy. To find what really brings us fulfillment, we must tune inward and connect with ourselves. To establish real relationships with others, we must show our true selves to the outside world instead of hiding behind a curated existence.

Who Benefits? Not You.

Maria has spent her life being polite and nice. She is self-sufficient and doesn't voice many wants and needs. She has followed the script and worked hard. She is a good girl, a good mom, a good daughter, a good coworker, and a good friend.

Based on what you know from this book so far, who do you think has benefited from Maria being small and polite, taking care of everyone else, being high-achieving and ultra productive, and never expressing any wants or needs?

You guessed it: her son, parents, siblings, coworkers, company, clients, and ex-husband have all reaped the fruit of her hard work and self-sacrifice. Everyone but Maria. Sure, there are moments when Maria feels good about the work she is doing and how she has contributed to the world. But more often than not, she is exhausted, depleted, and burned out.

Sound familiar?

As we've already mentioned, most of us have internalized the role of being an uber-productive good girl whose worth comes from the outside. We get hooked in because we mistakenly believe these roles define us and our worth. And, of course, the world isn't going to change—not overnight, anyway. It wants and needs us to stay in these roles, to stay in our boxes, *because the world is the main beneficiary of our self-sacrifice.*

These systems lead to our slow and steady self-abandonment over time, and neither Maria nor you can single-handedly change the systems in place or the demands that are placed upon women in our culture. There isn't a magic bullet that will dismantle these systems or a magic pill that will inoculate you from their influence entirely, but there is a powerful shield that can protect you and help you hold onto yourself: self-compassion. We've witnessed the profound impact of self-compassion firsthand—both with our clients and in our own lives.

Tuning In: Self-Compassion

Imagine you sit down for coffee with a good friend. She tells you she has had a horrible week. She shares about a fight she had with her partner, the "disastrous" mistake she made at work, and her lack of motivation, which has led her to oversleep and skip a few social commitments. Her lip starts to quiver, and you see her eyes begin to well up with tears. She tells you that she is so overwhelmed and that she feels like she's failing at everything.

As she is speaking, you feel yourself soften with care and concern. You feel immense empathy and warmth for your dear friend, and what you want more than anything is to alleviate her suffering. You attentively track what she is saying and respond with all sorts of understanding verbal and nonverbal responses: You nod your head, lean forward slightly as she talks, and gasp with "Oh no" at the right moments. You reach across the table to take her hand or pop up to give her a big hug. You are fully present, right there with her. You tell her you are so sorry it's been such an awful week, and you really mean it.

Most of us would respond with similar compassion in this situation. We have an easy time accessing compassion for the people we love, especially when we see them hurt and suffering.

Unfortunately, it can be much harder to tap into compassion for ourselves. When we practice self-compassion, we offer *ourselves* care. Not because we have "earned" it, but simply because we are suffering.

Both professionally and personally, we have found self-compassion to be the most powerful tool for a life filled with connection, peace, and ease. Indeed, the benefits of self-compassion are numerous.[30, 31] The more self-compassion we have, the greater our well-being. We are more positive, happier, and more satisfied with our lives. Self-compassion improves our relationships, makes us physically healthier, and fosters hope, gratitude, curiosity, and vitality. People with more self-compassion are wiser and more emotionally intelligent, and they are more motivated, conscientious, and resilient. In addition, self-compassion decreases shame and improves mental health, which means less depression, anxiety, fear, and stress.

We're not kidding when we say self-compassion is a magical superpower. It is one of the most powerful therapeutic tools we have encountered! It is truly *the* secret sauce.

Kristin Neff, the researcher who put self-compassion on the mainstream map, outlines three core components of self-compassion: mindfulness, self-kindness, and common humanity.[32] First, we must be mindful of our suffering—we must first notice and be aware of it—before we can harness compassion. Second, self-compassion entails meeting ourselves with care and kindness, rather than judgment and control. We trade in the whip of self-flagellation for a caring arm wrapped around our shoulders. Lastly, we recognize our common humanity. This is the idea that we are not alone. We all suffer, we all make mistakes, and we all mess up. This is part of being human.

Self-compassion is a core skill in staying connected to ourselves. When we show up for ourselves with kindness, rather than judgment, we're better able to tolerate uncomfortable feelings and difficult experiences. In turn, we more effectively support and care for ourselves. In other words, when we can harness self-compassion, we are far less likely to abandon ourselves.

As we move into the next chapter, here are some concrete exercises to help you practice self-compassion.

Do Try This at Home

#1: Tap into Self-Compassion

When you find yourself suffering in some way—when you're upset, sad, worried, angry—or when you notice self-judgment, stop and ask yourself these questions:

- What do I need now to alleviate my suffering?
- What can I do to tend to myself at this moment?
- How can I help myself right now?
- What do I truly need right now?

A great way to connect with compassion is to ask yourself, *What would I say to a friend?* Often, we're much kinder to the people we love than to ourselves, so thinking about it in the third person enables us to better access our internal compassion.

#2: Choose Supportive Words and Mantras

The way we speak to ourselves can either move us closer to or farther away from self-compassion. To move toward self-compassion, use words that are warm, supportive, and encouraging: "Ouch." "Oh, darling, you are suffering." "This is a painful moment. Pain is a part of being alive." "May I accept myself just as I am." "This is really hard." "This really sucks." "I'm already enough, just as I am."

#3: Place Your Hands on Your Body

When we gently place our hands on our bodies, we can better access compassion because this act, in and of itself, is a nonverbal behavior that, for many humans, automatically and subconsciously conveys kindness and care. Try any of the following:

- Place your hands over your heart.

- Place your hands on your belly.
- Put one hand on your heart and the other on your belly.
- Cradle your cheeks with your hands.
- With your back straight, place a fist over your chest, then place the other hand over your fist.
- Give yourself a hug (you can even rock a little as you do this!).
- Hold your own hand.

#4: Keep These Practices at the Top of Your Mind This Week

- Put a reminder on a sticky note and place it on your steering wheel.
- Write yourself a note on your bathroom mirror in dry-erase marker.
- Snap a picture of one of these practices and set it as the background of your phone.

Chapter 3

How We Abandon Ourselves

Alyssa hates the dating apps almost as much as she hates the fact that she can't seem to quit texting her ex-boyfriend, Brad. Right before their college graduation, Brad asked Alyssa to marry him, but she refused to settle for the small-town life Brad dreamed of creating with her. At the time, she had just landed a competitive job at a prestigious consulting firm across the country in New York City. Alyssa begged Brad to come with her, but it simply wasn't the future he wanted.

After two years in New York, Brad continues to provide comfort when Alyssa feels lonely, which is pretty much all the time. She has one friend from work, Sabrina, but they have not seen each other much outside of work since Sabrina started dating a new guy four months ago. Alyssa's mom keeps pressuring her to find a boyfriend—someone who, in her mom's words, is "successful, driven, and able to provide for you more than Brad ever could."

When Alyssa finds out Brad has been seeing someone for the last six months, a fact he has conveniently left out when they've connected over the phone, she is devastated. Alyssa knows the only way to finally move on from Brad is to block him on social media and stop answering his calls and texts, but she cannot bring herself to do it. She wonders, *What is wrong with me? When did I become so weak?*

Alyssa is so disappointed in who she has become. She was an athlete in high school and college—strong, focused, and goal oriented. She longs for the sense of belonging she once had with her teammates, who have all moved on with their lives. She knows she needs friends who live close by, but she has no idea where to meet people or how to make friends as an adult.

Throughout Alyssa's entire life, she has been working for the next thing. She has been propelled by her desire to succeed, and it has paid off, at least on paper. However, now that she's on her own, she wonders if she will ever feel like she's finally "arrived."

Many of you reading this book might relate to Alyssa's struggle. You did all the "right" things, yet you still long for more. In our experience, this feeling is the breeding ground for the four types of self-abandonment, which we will outline in the next section.

The Four Types of Personal Self-Abandonment

Getting Stuck in Our Heads

Beginning about 5 p.m. every Sunday, Alyssa reliably falls victim to the "Sunday scaries." Instead of being able to relax and enjoy what remains of her weekend, she starts dreading the week ahead. *Oh, God, something's going to go wrong at work tomorrow. Did I leave something out of that report I wrote last week? I really should spend some time on the dating apps tonight. But what's the point? Nothing's going to work out.* The thoughts, lists, and worries in her head go on and on, rapid-fire and ceaseless. She feels restless and overwhelmed, simultaneously depleted and worked up. So much for a peaceful Sunday evening.

Maybe you can relate to this feeling of constantly being stuck in your own head. It's easy to get lost in thinking, analyzing, worrying, ruminating, obsessing, or fixating. Whether you get caught in regret, fear, anxiety, self-judgment, or overwhelm, these constant thought loops are exhausting. This can lead you to overfocus on tasks, to-dos, and check boxes—getting bogged down with all your "shoulds," "oughts," and "musts."

You can imagine how destructive this can be over time. When we are in our heads, we ignore everything below our necks. We are so focused on our thoughts that we ignore our actual physical bodies, our sensations, our emotions, and our intuition. We become disconnected and disembodied, like a head floating in space.

There are definite payoffs to this behavior. If we are living as disembodied heads, we get to avoid feeling emotions, we feel more in control, and there's a sense of accomplishment or pride. We are getting *so much done*, all while being able to avoid some of the general discomfort that comes from living in our bodies and fully inhabiting our lives.

Don't get us wrong—spending time in our heads is not all bad. If analyzing and thinking are your default strategies for coping, it's likely that your cognitive abilities have served you well in many areas of your life. You get shit done, you're a master of keeping things (your life, everyone else's lives) on track and running smoothly, and you're probably also high-achieving, which can really stoke your confidence and self-worth. The problem arises when you spend too much time in your head—when you over-rely on thinking, planning, analyzing, and figuring it out—at the expense of listening to and trusting yourself on a deeper level.

Being disconnected from your body has a price. For starters, it is mentally draining, leading to exhaustion and burnout. It's hard to think your way out of overthinking. Being stuck in your head can make you feel overwhelmed and powerless, which makes it hard to be present. If you are talking with a friend or watching TV with your child, and you're engaged in endless chatter in your head, you're not going to be paying close attention to the person or activity before you. Instead of feeling focused and calm, you will likely feel constricted, frantic, urgent, and distracted.

The way we see it, the largest cost of being stuck in our heads is that we miss out on the valuable wisdom that comes from being fully embodied. So, how do we get unstuck? By simply acknowledging our thoughts without getting caught up in them. We notice our thoughts as they arise—without labeling them as "good" or "bad" or "right" or "wrong"—and allow them to come and go instead of becoming attached to them. This enables us to remain connected with our physical sensations, emotions, and intuition. When we are connected to our *entire* experience, we have more clarity about who we are and what we want and need. This enables us to access our IGS and make decisions, both big and small, that are aligned with our authentic selves.

The path out of our heads begins with connecting with our bodies—the wonderful, rich, and sometimes scary life below our necks. We access this through tuning in, which we will discuss in more depth later in this chapter.

Numbing

Over time, Alyssa stumbles across a few ways to take the edge off her "Sunday scaries." When her thoughts start to rev up, she reaches for a glass or three of wine. She turns on a show while scrolling through social media on her phone. Several hours can pass in this vegetative trance. Many times, she falls asleep on the couch, only to wake up exhausted and slightly hungover the following day.

Numbing is a mindless default setting that happens to all of us in one way or another. Have you noticed you're more likely to numb out when you're feeling emotionally overwhelmed, burned out, or exhausted? When we numb ourselves, we do not have to be present for who we are, how we feel, what's going on in our lives, or the people around us.

We humans are very creative in our methods for numbing out, which can include abusing alcohol or drugs, scrolling endlessly on social media, binge watching TV shows, overeating or undereating, shopping online, and oversleeping, just to name a few. We may turn to any number of behaviors to simply duck out of our lives for a bit. Most of us don't intentionally choose numbing as a coping strategy; it just kind of happens. We simply slide into our method of choice and zone out.

The problem with numbing is that we don't usually feel better afterward. Oftentimes, we feel worse. In fact, numbing tends to make us feel depleted, groggy, and out of sorts. When we don't give ourselves permission for proper rest, we may resort to numbing to get something that *feels* like rest. Scrolling mindlessly while simultaneously watching TV may look like "rest," but it isn't truly restorative. In addition, when we numb ourselves in response to difficult situations or emotions, we often neglect to return to the original issue that triggered our discomfort, which can lead us to avoid situations and emotions that truly need our attention.

When her son was in high school, Maria, our fifty-year-old friend from chapter two, received a notification that he was failing algebra and might not be able to graduate on time. Overwhelmed by the myriad emotions that began to arise, she grabbed a bag of chips and plopped down in front of the computer. Instead of dealing with this very real crisis, she lost herself in online shopping, as it was much easier to search for a good face cream than to tackle the anger and fear she felt over her son's potentially disrupted future.

When emotions are high—when we have strong feelings, are flustered, or are overwhelmed—it is hard to think clearly. In such moments, we don't really do the best problem-solving and decision-making. Big, intense emotions interfere with these higher-level, frontal-lobe cognitive processes. For example, Maria's numbing allowed her to escape her feelings of anger and fear, but it short circuited her ability to emotionally process and cope with the situation. She was operating on autopilot, without awareness or intention. This is what numbing does. It creeps in and makes us tune out and disconnect.

Of course, it isn't always a bad thing to disconnect from our lives for a bit. Especially in stressful situations or in times of trauma, we may need to take a time out. Sometimes, we need a moment to regroup and recalibrate. We might need a distraction, which affords time and space for our emotions and nervous system to settle. We psychologists call this "coming back to baseline." But how do we do that in a way that is conscious and intentional, without avoiding important issues, and where we feel better afterward?

We do so by *connecting* with ourselves, *noticing* when we need a distraction, and then making the *conscious choice* to step away and allow our emotions to simmer down. After we come back to baseline, we can directly address the issue at hand, if needed, later on. We stay connected to ourselves by tuning in, noticing what we want or need, and deliberately caring for ourselves to meet that want or need. When we intentionally rest when we're tired, pick up a captivating work of fiction to read when we're bored, or take a quick walk outside when we're stressed, we usually notice we feel better afterward.

As Maria has become more connected to herself, she has found that she can replace some of her numbing behaviors with intentional distraction. For example, when her now college-aged son informed her that he might be placed on academic probation next semester, she connected to herself and noticed, *Wow, my emotions are really high. I'm so frustrated! I don't know what to do next, but I do know if I get on the phone with him right now, my anger will get the best of me. I don't want to say something I'll regret. I need a minute to calm my nervous system.* She consciously made the decision to give herself the next hour for some online shopping and a warm bath. She then jotted down some notes with questions for her son and brainstormed possible ways to help if he was placed on academic probation. The next morning, she called her son to discuss his options with a clearer head.

As we've mentioned, mindless numbing and intentional distraction can look very similar on the outside, but they feel very different on the inside. The key difference is that numbing fails to effectively address our underlying wants and needs, and we don't usually feel any better when we slip out of numbing behaviors. Distraction, on the other hand, allows us to take a break when we need it and in a way that gives us more of what we need. In other words, distraction helps us stay connected, whereas numbing leads to self-abandonment.

Characteristics of Numbing	Characteristics of Distraction
• Disconnected • Unintentional • Unconscious • Draining • Used to avoid	• Connected • Intentional • Conscious • Restorative • Used to cope

The Quest for Self-Improvement

There's nothing wrong with wanting to improve ourselves. In fact, working toward goals that increase our life's meaning and purpose can improve our happiness and well-being.[33] Our quest for self-improvement is helpful when it comes from a connected place, when it's focused on learning and growth, and when it aligns with our values and priorities. Under these circumstances, our improvements come from a place of love and help us feel and live better.

On the other hand, it's difficult to remain tuned into ourselves when we feel like there is something innately "wrong" with us that we need to make "right" or something about us that is "broken" and needs to be "fixed." We end up believing we must fundamentally change ourselves to belong, have value, or be worthy. When not-enoughness drives our quest for self-improvement, we're likely to abandon ourselves.

Let's take Maria for example. Maria can trace one of her quests for self-improvement back to a thought she had while swimming in her neighborhood pool: *What would happen if I didn't eat dinner tonight? Would I look better in this swimsuit if I swam more and ate less?*

She was eight years old.

At such a young age, Maria didn't have the words for "diet culture" or an awareness of its insidious nature, but she had already internalized the message that society places a higher value on bodies that are thin. Since then, Maria has spent much of her life trying to shrink her body down to the "right" size to fit in and belong. She has viewed her body as "broken" every time her yo-yo dieting didn't work.

Thankfully, this story has a happy ending. One day, after a lifetime of obsessing over her food intake and her body, she couldn't take it anymore. She was cranky, hungry, and fighting through the mental fog that comes from not feeding one's body properly.

Do you know what she did? *She simply decided to stop*. It felt like such a rebellious act. She'd spent her entire life fighting these feelings, pushing past her hunger and discomfort, and berating herself for not measuring up. She had simply had enough of the self-loathing.

So, what changed? In a word: self-compassion.

Maria was able to shift her focus from self-improvement to self-compassion and change her mindset from "I must lose weight to be enough" to "I am enough just as I am." After a lifetime of believing that her enoughness was based on her body size, the idea felt totally radical. It was a total paradigm shift to believe that her body could really be enough, that *she* could really be enough just as she was.

Of course, Maria's experience is not unique. Many women believe their enoughness depends on aspects of their physical appearance, and weight loss isn't the only multibillion-dollar industry that thrives as a result. Countless businesses profit when we base our worth on external standards of beauty, including the health, wellness, cosmetic, and beauty industries. When advertising tells us that we must look a certain way to be enough, we'll do anything we can to measure up. But we know that what's good for these businesses is not good for us. When we believe that our worth and value are contingent upon the way we look, when we believe that our enoughness comes from outside of us, we abandon our authentic selves.

Our quest for self-improvement is not limited to our physical appearance. Working toward accolades and success in other aspects of our lives—whether it comes to our educational achievement, job performance, or financial success—can also be driven by not-enoughness. Obviously, it makes total sense you'd want to succeed at work. We do too! However, if the only way for you to feel like you are "enough" is to become a partner or join the C-suite, you may be prioritizing work to the point that you're ignoring other important aspects of your identity. And we hate to break it to you, but even if you *do* make partner or reach the C-suite, the not-enoughness you feel will likely still exist, and you'll have to find the next goal to chase.

The bottom line is that we abandon ourselves when our quest for self-improvement feels never-ending; our efforts and progress are never enough. We know we are in this dangerous territory when we constantly compare, compete, and strive to compensate for our underlying sense of not-enoughness. Again, working toward a worthy goal that aligns with our values can serve to keep us grounded and come from a connected place. But when the work we do toward those goals drives us to become rigid, constricted, and obsessive with our efforts, we know there is a problem.

If we're driven by the big black hole of not-enoughness inside of us, no amount of self-improvement will ever be enough—no weight loss, job promotion, or self-care hack for a better life. We might get temporary relief when we see a tangible "improvement," but this will not fill the hole of not-enoughness. Instead, we must learn to tend to our not-enoughness with compassion when it arises, leaning into the knowing that we are actually already enough, just as we are.

Willful Disengagement

Isabel, our thirty-something friend from chapter one, awoke with a start one Sunday morning as she heard the kiddos arguing downstairs. "It's *my* turn, William! You lost that round! Give me the PlayStation controller!" Then came the sound of shattering glass and crying. She glanced over at George who was snoring loudly, blissfully unaware of the chaos. She dragged herself out of bed and trudged downstairs. "What in the world is going on?" Isabel demanded with a raised voice. Immediately, the kids began pointing fingers at one another. "I don't want to hear it. Go to your rooms *now*!"

This is not how Isabel had imagined her Sunday morning would begin, but these interruptions to her rest and her need to mediate the kids' disagreements were becoming more and more frequent. As Isabel began sweeping up the broken picture-frame pieces, she became even more irritated. *I am so sick and tired of dealing with the constant bickering. Can't I get ONE day to sleep in, even just a little? Doesn't George notice? Does he even care? Honestly, why would he when I'm literally always around to clean up everyone else's mess?*

Isabel's frustration had reached a boiling point. She went upstairs, grabbed a T-shirt and sweats, and went into the bathroom to change, slamming the door. When she exited the bathroom, George awoke groggily, "What's going on? Are you going to grab donuts for the kids?" Isabel glared back at him icily, "Nope." She grabbed her keys and left the house without saying another word.

As Isabel tried to cope with the unpleasant start to her morning, she demonstrated what is called *willful disengagement*: She responded to the situation at hand by intentionally removing herself from it. We may opt for willful disengagement when we don't agree with what is happening to us, we feel uncomfortable, or we have difficulty tolerating our emotions and the current situation. Rather than directly asking for what we need or communicating a boundary with others, we simply stop participating in the moment. Rather than staying connected to ourselves and our values or trying to collaborate with others to find a workable solution, we throw our hands up and retreat into ourselves. We believe that we are "right" and know what "should" be done, so we physically or emotionally separate ourselves by detaching, withdrawing, or stonewalling. At its core, willful disengagement is an attempt to set limits and meet our needs, but we end up doing so in a way that is indirect and maladaptive.

Willful disengagement ultimately stems from our needs not being met. In the previous example, Isabel had two needs: (1) to have an easier and more peaceful morning and (2) to have George step up and take a more active role in parenting. Completely reasonable, right? She desperately wanted her husband to recognize her needs, and leaving home certainly forced him into a more active parenting role in that moment. However, the larger issue of equitable division of responsibilities remained.

We've heard several examples of willful disengagement from our clients (and each other), including leaving a dirty dish on the counter to see if someone ever takes notice and washes it or letting the trash overflow to see if someone might care enough to empty the bin. At some point, we've probably all used these types of nonverbal behaviors to send the message "Get a clue and help out" or "I'm exhausted and I'm opting out. I'm done." Although we might think we're leaving obvious hints with these behaviors, we aren't being very clear or direct when we communicate our needs in a passive-aggressive way. That's the problem with willful disengagement: We don't directly express our feelings or openly communicate what we want or need, so we run a greater risk of not being heard or understood.

When we don't get our needs met time and time again, we experience underlying emotions such as frustration, anger, and resentment. As we've discussed, women are often discouraged from directly expressing these types of feelings, so these strong emotions often end up coming out sideways, so to speak. These untended emotions build and build until something has to give, like the proverbial straw that broke the camel's back. In Isabel's case, her frustration and resentment grew over time until she couldn't ignore them anymore. If you are experiencing frustration, your frustration is valid. Frustration is often a product of repeated self-abandonment. Resentment and anger often serve as a reminder that you need to tend to and prioritize yourself. We all need to disengage from time to time, but there are more effective ways to do that, one of which involves setting effective boundaries.

We are big proponents of setting effective boundaries, which we will talk about much more in chapter six. Clearly communicating what you will or won't do in a connected, intentional, and kind way is a great way to set a boundary. Expecting others to read your mind and then throwing your hands up and dramatically saying, "I'm done!" is not. Asking for help is an effective way to get your needs met. Sulking and giving someone the silent treatment for not being able to anticipate your needs and wants is not. Being open to hearing alternative solutions is an effective way to collaborate and solve problems. Insisting that it's "your way or the highway" is not.

If willful disengagement is your MO from time to time, try not to beat yourself up. Lots of us choose to dig in and say nothing rather than speak up and ask for help. Sometimes, people get it. They step up and help when they see us in our silent state of misery or fury. But most of the time, people don't get it, and we are left disappointed. And constant disappointment eventually builds into resentment, which can have a detrimental effect on our relationships, not to mention the continual pattern of abandoning our own needs, wants, and values.

So, while we admit that willful disengagement might feel good in the moment (because, hey, who doesn't like getting their way and feeling right or justified?), it comes with long-term negative consequences that affect our sense of self, our ability to get what we want and need in a healthy way, and our relationships in general.

Instead, we can stay connected to ourselves by practicing effective boundary setting, asking for help, and tending to ourselves with compassion when things don't go our way. This might be a hard habit to break. Start by paying attention to your internal experiences, especially during times of discomfort and frustration, and accept the pieces that you cannot change, which is exactly what we are going to talk about next.

Acceptance

As psychologists, we consider acceptance to be a vital component of a connected life. Acceptance is about allowing our internal experiences to be just as they are, without judging or immediately trying to change them. In essence, it's about making room for what we feel, even when these feelings involve discomfort, and being willing to have all the experiences without attempting to fix, control, or avoid them.

Acceptance does not mean that we like, approve of, want, or tolerate all our experiences in life. Rather, it means that we allow space and have compassion for whatever arises. Acceptance allows us to acknowledge the reality of the situation and intentionally respond to *what is* rather than getting lost in how we think it should be or how we wish it were.

Of course, acceptance is easier said than done. See if you can relate to Ruby.

Ruby had just sat down to dinner to celebrate her seventy-second birthday when her cell phone rang. It was her son, Marcus. He'd been laid off (again) and needed help (again). Ruby to the rescue.

"Marcus, I'm so sorry. You just started that job and I can't believe they let you go after two short months. Yes, of course, I can lend you the money for your car payment. How are the kids? Do they need anything?" Ruby's significant other, Paul, sighed and shook his head as he listened to Ruby's end of the conversation.

Ruby's friends and family would describe her as loving, caring, dependable, and selfless. She'd taken care of others since a young age. Being the eldest of seven children in a small rural town, her parents relied on her to help tend to her younger siblings, including a younger brother who had many medical issues. Her experience caring for a family member with severe illness led her to work in the nursing field, which she did for forty-five years before she retired. Her most important value has always been service to others.

Ruby never outwardly complained about her son's instability, but the unpredictability and chaos of Marcus's life had taken its toll. Each time she helped Marcus, Ruby felt short-term relief, but she also knew it was only a matter of time before Marcus would come to her to bail him out again. Ruby had great difficulty accepting that Marcus was taking advantage of her generosity.

Acceptance is easy when it's things we like or want. Got a huge raise at work? Terrific! You won a raffle prize at an auction? Congratulations! Kids made the honor roll? Fantastic! It makes sense that when life goes our way, things are easy to accept.

But you know as well as we do that life throws us curveballs that can make acceptance more challenging. In our private practices, one area where we see the most difficulty with acceptance is in all the many ups and downs that come with parenting.

If you're a parent, think back to when your child was born. What were your hopes, dreams, and expectations for them? Now think about where you and your child are now. How are you aligned and where do you differ? Maybe their sexual orientation or gender identity is different from what you had imagined or assumed. Maybe you discovered that they have experimented with drugs when you've never done anything harder than caffeine. Maybe they have a completely different political ideology than you do and it's hard to fathom where that came from. Maybe they've been diagnosed with a learning disability or are neurodivergent when you breezed through school without a hitch.

Whatever the circumstance, it can be quite painful and scary as parents to allow our children to grow up and be the people they are meant to be. Acceptance means allowing our children to develop their own sense of self. It's loving them just *as they are* without pressuring them to change. When we do this, we're able to develop and maintain closeness.

If you're having difficulty accepting where your child is in life, you may need time and a safe space to grieve and work through any complicated emotions. However, know that talking to your child about your complicated feelings about them is not likely to go well, especially in the context of big and overwhelming emotions. You are unlikely to get the support you are looking for, and your child will likely be left feeling confused and hurt. Instead, you'll want to work through these emotions in the context of a close, trusted relationship or in a therapy setting. You deserve the opportunity to talk openly with other adults about your own, perhaps messy, feelings about what is happening in your child's life. It's incredibly important to process whatever emotions you might have about parenthood.

Every type of self-abandonment, from getting stuck in our heads to willfully disengaging, involves some aspect of non-acceptance. When we get stuck in our heads, we ruminate, worry, and obsessively problem-solve rather than accepting the difficult feelings we're experiencing. For example, we might ruminate about a difficult conversation we need to have with a friend, even though that doesn't change the reality that the conversation needs to occur. Similarly, when we willfully disengage, we don't accept reality but try to fit reality into what we think should be occurring. For example, we might leave dirty dishes in the sink for days in the hopes that someone will "notice" and take care of them, but that won't necessarily lead to quickly cleaned dishes.

Refusing to accept reality does not actually change reality; it simply increases suffering. If your child's teachers are concerned that she may have a learning disability, rejecting this reality will not change the situation. However, non-acceptance is likely to increase your and your daughter's suffering. If you remain convinced that she's just not trying hard enough in school, even as she claims to be trying as hard as possible, she's likely to feel misunderstood and defeated, and you may feel frustrated, anxious, and helpless as well. Neither you nor your daughter is going to be effective in this scenario.

In contrast, acceptance helps you discern whether there is a problem that needs to be solved. When you lean into acceptance, you sometimes discover that there's nothing for you to change or fix—the situation is out of your control. Acceptance also removes you from the position of being in charge, where you think you're the only one who knows what's best or right. It allows you to be with reality as it *is*, not what you wish it to be. This, in turn, allows you to settle, relax, and move forward rather than getting stuck on "why" something has happened. Trust us when we say that this is a liberating concept that helps you stay connected to yourself.

Of course, there will be times when accepting a situation may move you directly into problem-solving mode. For example, let's say you notice that when you drink alcohol, you do things you later regret, don't sleep well, and feel crappy the next day. Accepting that alcohol isn't working for you could be just the motivation you need to change your drinking behaviors. Starting with acceptance means you don't waste time putting your head in the sand or wearing yourself out trying to see the situation differently. In this situation, you are able to jump in and start tackling the problem. To put it bluntly, acceptance gets you to stop fighting your pain, suppressing unwanted emotions, and catastrophizing about not getting your way so that you can experience more clarity about how to solve the problem while staying true to yourself.

Have we convinced you of the power of acceptance? We hope so! Assuming so, you're probably wondering where to begin incorporating this practice into your daily life. In the next section, we'll talk about how acceptance works in tandem with tuning in to yourself and listening to the whole of your internal experience.

Tuning In: Learning to Listen to and Trust Yourself

Self-abandonment happens when we disconnect from ourselves. Conversely, we can connect to ourselves by tuning in and learning to listen to and trust ourselves. See if you can relate to this example from Maria, who is already carrying so much in her busy life.

During her therapy session, Maria began sharing about the latest difficulties in her relationship with her mom. She spoke loudly and rapidly, barely taking a breath between statements: "I'm so . . . ugh . . . I don't even know. I can't believe she is so self-centered! I mean, I call to tell her about my promotion at work and she basically cuts me off to talk about her latest doctor's appointment. She went on and on for twenty minutes about herself and asked nothing about me. I just don't get why she can't be supportive and interested in what I do. Interested in *me*. Why do I even bother? My friends tell me she's my mom and she won't be around forever. They say I shouldn't be so upset. But isn't a mom supposed to be your biggest cheerleader?"

Our first response as psychologists in situations like this is often to help our clients tune in to themselves. In response to a client like Maria, we might say: "Take a moment to tune in. What do you notice in your body? What emotions are you feeling? What's happening in your head?"

We repeat these prompts often in our work as therapists. When clients show up to sessions with lots of overwhelming feelings like Maria's, these questions can help them tune in to their own emotions. When a client is unsure of what decision to make, these words can remind them to look inside and access their IGS for clarity. When a client gets caught in judgment and self-criticism, or in apathy and numbness, these simple phrases can help them access more curiosity and openness. When a client seems stuck in their head or disconnected from themselves, these prompts can help them connect to self.

In essence, these prompts—and really, any form of slowing down and tuning inward—bring us back to ourselves.

Remember in chapter one when we talked about the tendency to look outside ourselves as a core feature underlying self-abandonment? This is when we let our EGS overpower our IGS. When we tune in, we turn the volume up on our IGS. We look inward so we can learn to listen to and trust ourselves.

Before we go any further, let's take a moment to try this practice of tuning in:

- Invite yourself to slow down. All the way down. Take a deep, calming breath.
- Place your hands over your heart or on your belly. What do you notice in your body? What emotions are you feeling? What's happening in your head?
- That's it—you did it! You tuned in!

We're curious: Did you actually try this? Or did you perhaps think, *I'll come back to that when I have more time*? If you blew right past this exercise, we can relate! In our busy lives, with way too much to do, it can be hard to take a moment to stop and listen to ourselves. But the truth is that it is impossible to connect with ourselves when we're frantically rushing or full steam in productivity mode. To help you get into the practice of tuning in, the following section walks you through the steps involved in this process.

Step 1: Slow Down

The first step to tuning in is to *slow down*. This is all about setting the stage—getting into the right position and frame of mind.

You can tune in anywhere, at any time. It's a very portable practice! When you're starting out, it can be helpful to find a quiet space, free of distractions or chaos. Put your phone on silent, or better yet, put it in another room. You can think about finding the 3 S's: stillness, silence, and solitude.

Then find a comfortable position, seated, lying, or standing. Test out different locations and positions. Once you're situated, we recommend closing your eyes, as this can help you get centered. Then connect with yourself, simply noticing who you are in the moment and listening to what your body is telling you. Because you're human, you'll get distracted as you practice tuning in. Your attention will wander. When you notice this happening, gently bring your awareness back to the present moment and back to yourself.

We encourage you to make this practice your own. We've seen our clients adopt this practice in many ways, each unique and customized to them. Some busy moms get to the carpool lane a few minutes early to have a quiet moment to connect with themselves before the after-school chaos begins. Others steal a quiet moment alone while the kids are getting ready for bed. We know women who sneak to the bathroom during happy hour for a few quick breaths. Many women also enjoy a more formal tuning-in practice, setting alarms and having a dedicated space for quietly listening inward when they wake up, just before bed, or any time in between. The hardest part is remembering to make the time to pause and look inward, especially in a world with endless possible distractions.

So, once you've slowed down and are all settled, what do you do next?

Step 2: Tune Inward

The next step is to bring your awareness inward . . . to quite literally tune in and connect with your internal experience. Notice your thoughts, emotions, body sensations, and intuition. We're really aiming to connect with our bodies, rather than getting stuck in our heads. We get that this process might sound counterintuitive. How can we tune in without using our thinking brains? We can notice our thinking, but this is not really the time and space to *think*. Let's see if we can show you what we mean.

To avoid getting lost in our heads—with endless to-do lists, worries about what's to come, or replays of the past—it helps to start with an anchor to center us and connect us to ourselves. Here are some of our favorite options:

1. **Place your hands on your body.** Placing your hands on your body can facilitate tuning in because it literally helps you connect with and subsequently feel your physical body. Try putting both hands over your heart or one hand on your heart and the other on your belly.
2. **Find your feet.** Your feet are the farthest part of your body from your head, and life happens wherever your feet are. Bringing awareness to your physical feet is both a practice and a reminder to be in the present moment. You can do this from any position. If your feet are on the floor, you can move your weight to your toes, then to your heels, then to the outsides, then to the insides. You can then root down through your whole foot. Let yourself be firmly planted in this present moment.
3. **Focus on your breath.** The breath is always available, right there with you. You don't need any special props. You. Just. Breathe. Taking slow, deep breaths helps harness the parasympathetic nervous system, the part of the brain that helps settle and relax us. Focus on your inhales and exhales, letting your breath guide you inward to your body. We recommend slow and deep breaths. Place one hand on your chest and one on your belly. Breathe so that with each breath, you can feel your belly move in and out, rising with the in-breath and falling with the out-breath. Most often, we take shallow breaths, where only the hand on our chest will move. Instead, intentionally deepen your breath to move all the way into your belly and lower back.
4. **Practice gentle movement.** Sometimes, it's hard to sit still. Your body can feel wiggly and almost itchy. In such moments, some

gentle movement can greatly support your capacity to tune in. This might include stretching or doing some light yoga. You can use a lacrosse ball or foam roller to self-massage so that you can feel your body from the outside in. Neck rolls are fabulous too, and slow, mindful walking can help you center as well. In other words, you can use movement to bring you into yourself.

5. **Use a mantra.** Mantras are words or phrases that help you stay in the present moment and facilitate you coming into yourself. There are so many mantras to choose from! You can say "I have arrived" as you breathe in and "I am here" as you breathe out. Inhale "Peace" and exhale "Ease." Inhale "Just this moment" and exhale "Just this breath."
6. **Scan for body sensations, emotions, and thoughts.** As you tune inward, notice what's happening inside you. What sorts of body sensations are you experiencing? What emotions do you notice? Emotions are single words, like anxious, sad, scared, exhausted, or lonely. What do you notice about your thoughts? Is your mind quiet and calm, or busy with lots of racing thoughts?

The main goal is simply to show up for and connect with yourself. There is not a right or wrong way to do this, and we are not looking for any sort of "answer" or "aha" experience. You're just meeting yourself where you are.

Some of you might be wondering, *Wait, is this the same thing as meditation? Or mindfulness? They all sound a lot alike.* Yep! You nailed it! We most definitely consider tuning in under the umbrella of meditation and other contemplative approaches. Such ancient practices have been at the heart of spirituality and healing for centuries. We've tested them out in our own lives and in our clinical practices, and we strive to use these tools daily. We've noticed a direct correlation between our mental and emotional well-being and tuning in: The more consistently we tune in, the more peace and ease we feel inside. We feel better, and we cope better. They really do work.

For many people, slowing down and tuning inward can be uncomfortable at first. It's hard to sit with yourself and settle into your own skin. It takes practice. The more you do this, the easier it becomes and the more helpful it feels. However, even when we have a lot of practice, there are still days when it feels hard to tune in. That's simply part of the practice.

Let's return to our conversation with Maria about her frustrations with her mom. Maria was familiar with this practice, so when asked to tune in, she closed her eyes and took a deep breath. Her hands instinctively settled on her chest. Maria started to tear up, and she said, "I'm feeling really mad. And sad. I notice a tight, heavy ball in my chest. I was excited to share the news of my promotion with Mom, and I'm disappointed she didn't show up the way I wanted her to. I wish my dad was still alive. He always listened so well. I really miss him." Notice that Maria's statement didn't contain anything extra to muddy the water: no self-judgment, no negative thoughts, no worry about what her friends might think. She simply put words to what she noticed inside herself.

Slowing down and building awareness in this way facilitates a beautiful call-and-response loop: We tune in, notice what's happening, honor where we are and what we need, and make a plan to tend to ourselves well. Again, and again, and again. This iterative call-and-response loop builds self-trust, as it helps us develop or connect back to our relationship with ourselves. And when we have a strong relationship with ourselves—when we learn to listen to and trust ourselves—we plant strong roots of internal worth and value. Our worth comes from within, which is a much more powerful source of worth than looking to unstable external forces.

When we introduced the concept of tuning in to Alyssa, whom you met at the start of this chapter, she decided she was ready to give it a try instead of drinking wine and scrolling in response to her Sunday scaries.

She invested in a meditation cushion and transformed a corner of her apartment into a calming and peaceful area that contained candles, a few books of poetry, a lacrosse ball, and a fuzzy blanket. On this particular Sunday, she opted for a calming playlist to help set the mood. She lit the candles, grabbed the lacrosse ball, plopped down on her cushion, and threw the blanket across her lap. She began with some neck rolls and then used the lacrosse ball to massage her shoulder, neck, hands, and feet. She set the ball to the side after this gentle movement, feeling more settled and grounded in her body.

Alyssa then closed her eyes and placed one hand on her belly and one over her heart. She took some slow and deep breaths, letting the air move all the way into her belly and lower back. As she breathed, she anchored her awareness on her breath and repeated a mantra to herself, saying "I have arrived" as she breathed in and "I am here" as she breathed out.

Alyssa then shifted her awareness to her physical body and emotions. She noticed a cluster of anxiety and dread in her chest, which felt like a heavy, coarse rope knotted tightly, crowding out her lungs. She felt a heaviness in her stomach, like a sinking pit. She felt a pressure in her head, which she saw as all her thoughts racing around a track—going in infinite loops—at mad speeds. She almost felt dizzy observing this inside her. She felt tired and overwhelmed. Underneath all of this, she felt lonely and scared. Unfulfilled. Not enough. She observed the thoughts, *I can't do this anymore* and *This is not the life I want.*

Alyssa continued to breathe deeply through all of this. She noticed her experience with compassion. Having her hands resting gently on her body helped her better access this compassion and care. She realized, *Wow, there's a lot going on . . . a lot of uncomfortable things inside me. No wonder these quiet Sunday evenings are so hard. There's a lot bubbling to the surface.*

Alyssa had learned that the practice of tuning in was about listening and understanding, so she didn't rush to fix or problem-solve any of this. She just let it be. She made a concerted effort to make space for her whole experience and let it all be without judging it, stuffing it down, or pushing it away.

Remember, tuning in looks different for everyone and can be different for you each time you try it. There are so many possible ways to connect with yourself! Take a moment to reflect on Maria and Alyssa's examples of tuning in. Did anything about their experiences resonate with or inspire you? How can you personalize the practice of tuning in to fit with your own life? Practice being curious about what you might want to experiment with. Are there certain situations or moments in your day where you could benefit from slowing down and tuning in?

It's unavoidable that when you start integrating this practice into your daily life, issues will come to light that you will need to address. As simple as it sounds, tuning in can be difficult. Increasing self-awareness can be painful and hard. We will begin addressing those issues in the chapters ahead.

Until then, we invite you to start here. To slow down and develop more awareness. To stay grounded in the present moment, rather than getting lost in your head, numbing out, or disconnecting from yourself. By tuning in, you can connect with yourself and your direct experience—with what's actually happening in the moment. This is the opposite of abandoning yourself. It's staying awake to and for your life. However, the goal isn't to avoid all obstacles or to live every second of every day perfectly tuned in. That would be impossible. The key is to notice when you've stepped away—when you've abandoned yourself—and to give yourself the space and grace to come back to who you truly are.

Do Try This at Home

#1: Use an Anchor to Help You Tune In

Over the next week, find a few minutes in your schedule each day to practice tuning in. Experiment with the anchors listed earlier in this chapter: hands on body, find your feet, focus on your breath, gentle movement, use a mantra, or scan for body sensations, emotions, and thoughts.

#2: Find an Exit Ramp from Your Head

Whenever you notice you're stuck in your head, and thereby disconnected from yourself, take a few moments to drop down into your body:

- Take three slow, deep breaths.
- Focus on your five senses.
- Imagine watching the thoughts in your head from a distance. Perhaps you're at a train station and all your thoughts are the trains passing by. Or imagine your thoughts as leaves floating down a river or clouds passing through the sky.

#3: Slow Down

Pick one opportunity to slow down today. Maybe you erase an item from your to-do list, or you intentionally walk slower when moving from one point to the next, or you take a pause when you step outside to empty the trash. Use the moment of slowing down to look inward. Meet yourself right where you are.

Chapter 4

Under the Surface

Now that we've talked about the different ways we abandon ourselves, let's focus on what drives those behaviors so we can be more aware of them as they come up in our lives. What issues are lurking beneath the surface when we're getting stuck in our heads or numbing out? What motivates the quest for self-improvement, and what causes willful disengagement? In this chapter, we'll cover the four core issues that underlie self-abandonment: self-judgment; fear of discomfort; the desire to fix, plan, and control; and self-doubt.

The Core Issues Underlying Self-Abandonment

Self-Judgment

Most of us agree that we should refrain from being assholes to others, right? Yet, despite this, we often speak to *ourselves* in harsh, critical, and self-aggressive ways, ways in which we would never speak to a friend or even a stranger. There are many "technical" names for this behavior, including self-judgment, self-criticism, or negative self-talk, but we prefer to simply call it what it is: being an asshole to yourself. This can sound like:

- *I'm so fat and old. I've totally let myself go.*

- *I can't believe I skipped my workout to sleep in. I'm so lazy!*
- *Why the fuck can't I get my life together? I'm a total mess.*

For many of us, judgments occur automatically and unconsciously. We don't even realize we're doing it, yet we feel the impact emotionally. Remember Alyssa from the last chapter, who couldn't understand why she was feeling so hopeless and down on herself since cutting off contact with her ex-boyfriend? As she tuned in and got curious about what might be underneath these feelings, she discovered a slew of judgments that were driving her distress:

- *I'll never find anyone who loves me.*
- *I'm doomed to spend the rest of my life alone.*
- *I always fail at relationships. What's wrong with me?*

Inevitably, self-judgment makes us feel bad about ourselves: inadequate, not enough, worthless, weak, wrong, guilt-ridden, and like a failure. In addition, when we're already struggling, self-judgment reliably exacerbates our emotions, making it even harder to cope and function.[34] For instance, remember Maria, our fifty-year-old friend from chapter two? She was feeling worked up about a fight she had with her son. Before she knew it, self-judgments popped into her head: *I'm a horrible mother. I can't believe I lost my temper. I'm a disgrace.* These judgments made her feel even worse, as they added in a layer of shame and despair.

While tuning in can help us become more *aware* of our judgments, it doesn't make them disappear. In fact, in our clinical practices, we've noticed that clients tend to resist letting go of self-judgment. The most common barrier is the belief that we all need a whip of self-flagellation to keep ourselves in line and that without it, we'd fall apart. We've been conditioned to see self-judgment as a primary driver of motivation. But that is simply not the case. Often, when we're trapped in harsh self-judgment, we actually become *less* motivated and less confident. We become beat down, fearful, anxious, and constricted. And the self-abandonment continues.

During therapy sessions, we use the following anecdote to help clients understand the impact of self-judgment, especially when a client is insistent they need self-judgment to keep themselves in line:

> "Imagine you're babysitting a small girl named Eleanor. You're coloring together, and you've been instructed to ensure she colors inside the lines. Sweet Eleanor loves to color, though she's less concerned with staying inside the lines, so her coloring starts to venture outward. You react with judgment and in a loud and aggressive voice say, 'What in the world are you doing, Eleanor? Can't you follow a simple instruction? You're being so difficult!'"

As we describe this scenario, our clients inevitably cringe in horror and discomfort. Never once in all the years we've used this example have we had any client suggest that getting out the whip of judgment with Eleanor would be helpful, effective, or a good idea in any way.

As we continue discussing, we typically brainstorm three options that reflect how Eleanor might respond to such harsh criticism. In the first option, she bursts into tears because she feels hurt, sad, and scared. In the second option, she runs out of the room and refuses to ever color again. In the third option, she quickly and quietly complies, anxious and careful to only color inside the lines.

Can you relate to any of these responses in your own life?

The one good thing about the first option is that although Eleanor feels bad, she at least allows herself to feel the very real and expected emotions from encountering judgment. Many of us unconsciously and automatically sidestep these uncomfortable feelings with numbing behaviors or overproductivity.

We can't put the same positive spin on the second option. Eleanor's reaction cuts off joy, play, learning, and growth due to the belief that she isn't "enough" or isn't able to do it "right." This is when judgment shuts us down and causes us to disconnect from positive emotions and experiences.

In the third option, compliance leaves Eleanor riddled with fear and anxiety, feelings she will likely take with her long past this coloring activity. Yes, she has figured out what is expected of her and how to make everyone else happy. But it comes with a huge cost: She feels anxious and afraid, constricted and bound up. Many of our clients present to therapy with significant fear and anxiety, and we can often trace these symptoms back to underlying self-judgment.

In this example, Eleanor experiences judgment from an outside third party. But ultimately, this is a metaphor for how we judge ourselves. Each of us has a sweet child within who is just trying to live her best, joy-filled life, and each of us has a harsh critic who is perhaps trying to help us but who often does more harm than good. We experience the same repercussions of judgment when we're cruel to ourselves as when we are judged by someone else. When we get out our whip and fall into self-judgment, it's painful, shuts us down, and leads to fear, anxiety, and not-enoughness.

So, why are we so intent on helping women stop the constant cycle of self-judgment? *Because self-judgment paves the way for self-abandonment.* Constant self-criticism and self-judgment keep us stuck in despair instead of moving us toward the potential for change and growth.

We attempt to avoid this discomfort by jumping ship and disconnecting from ourselves. We get stuck in our heads, go on a quest for self-improvement, or engage in some sort of numbing or willful disengagement. Regardless of the path, judgment drives us to separate from ourselves and others. When we can instead shift to a nonjudgmental stance and harness compassion, so many doors of connection open to us.

Fear of Discomfort

As we mentioned in chapter one, one of the biggest drivers of self-abandonment is the urge to hide from discomfort. Discomfort is an unavoidable part of the human experience, but we often expend all kinds of energy trying to steer clear of any pain or suffering, whether that's *emotional* (embarrassment, anxiety, guilt, sadness, disappointment, anger), *cognitive* (disagreements over opinions that don't align with our own, difficult conversations around hot topics such as religion or politics, setting boundaries with others), or *physical* (pain, stress, tension, unpleasant physiological reactions). So many of us feel ill-equipped or unwilling to cope with and manage discomfort. In his book *Will and Spirit*, author and psychiatrist Gerald May writes:

> We are becoming increasingly unwilling to feel sad or afraid or to experience any other uncomfortable feeling. We ought to be able, we assume, to manage ourselves into efficient, self-actualizing, and almost constant happiness. If I feel bad, then, it means I have failed at managing myself. I must then try to get back on top of my feelings, back in *control*. . . . Bad feelings are to be eradicated with the utmost efficiency. Good feelings are to be maintained and amplified. (p. 7)[35]

We are often so afraid of experiencing discomfort that we put ourselves through all kinds of acrobatics to avoid it: staying busy, people-pleasing, overdrinking, overeating, overworking, avoiding, distracting, numbing, ignoring our desires, playing it safe, or stuffing down our truths. However, when we hide from discomfort for too long, our worlds become smaller. We become stuck and rigid, forgoing flexibility and new experiences, which can lead to a tedious, dull, and sometimes painful existence filled with regret.

It's easy to tell ourselves that we aren't hurting anyone with this behavior. But that is simply not the case.

Let's imagine you have a teenager at home who seems to have great difficulty waking up in time for school. For years, you've been his personal alarm clock. He'll be graduating in two short years, so you know he needs to be responsible for his own sleep-wake schedule. However, every time you think about letting him take over the responsibility and possibly struggling, you start to experience discomfort. Your mind races. *What if he's late to school? Even worse, what if he misses school? What if there's an important assignment or test that he won't be able to make up if he's absent? How will this affect his chances for getting into a good college if his grades slip because he's constantly tardy? And I have to be at work early, so how will he get to school if he's late anyway?*

It can be very difficult letting go of the habit of being your teen's time savior. In this situation, if you continue along the lines of "rescuing" your child because you're uncomfortable and worried about his discomfort, you aren't actually helping him at all. You're losing sight of your bigger value of helping him grow, eventually becoming an independent, resilient young adult. You're also not being a great model for how to simultaneously tolerate discomfort and do the things that are important to you.

Here's the truth: When we take risks, expose ourselves to novel situations, and step outside of our comfort zones, we *are* going to feel some discomfort. It might be a feeling of fear. It might be full-fledged terror. It could be sadness, uncertainty, anxiety, or insecurity—almost any emotion! If you're human, discomfort is universal and to be expected. The good news is that discomfort often leads to learning and growth.

Ruby, our seventy-two-year-old widowed mom from the last chapter, has had a long history of hiding from discomfort. When Ruby was married, she often dealt with her uncomfortable feelings about her husband's drinking by minimizing his behavior: *He just drinks to relax. He's such a hard worker. He doesn't drink every day. He can go weeks without even drinking at all.* Rather than face an uncomfortable conversation about his drinking, Ruby accommodated his drinking behaviors by canceling dinner plans with friends when he had too much to drink or attempting to alleviate his stress in hopes that it would help him not want to drink. More generally, Ruby tried to outrun distress, both for herself and everyone else around her, by becoming overly involved in her loved ones' lives and rescuing them from their own problems.

What happens when you experience unpleasant thoughts or difficult emotions? Do you try your best to distract yourself? Do you push the thoughts and feelings away? Do you get sucked into the black hole of rumination? Do you believe you have to "do something" to fix what you're thinking or feeling? All these reactions are completely understandable, especially given our society's emphasis on cultivating happiness over tolerating discomfort.

There's nothing wrong with wanting to be happy, but it often comes at the price of ignoring or avoiding discomfort. This tendency to avoid the uncomfortable can become an inflexible habit, which can be problematic when we're faced with uncontrollable, unchangeable, or uncertain situations. And inflexible habits really narrow our worlds and cause us to lose touch with who we are, ultimately causing us to abandon ourselves.

So, if we're really *living* life, meaning we're living fully and authentically, we're going to experience discomfort. That needs to be okay.

Ultimately, we cannot hide from discomfort. Instead, we must make room for all our feelings, even the uncomfortable ones. Our feelings help us remain grounded and connected to who we are and who we want to be.

The Desire to Fix, Plan, and Control

The desire to fix, plan, and control is really the desire to do something—anything—to manage our environment. When we interpret uncomfortable feelings as a call to action, it's easy to jump right into "doing" mode. We try to fix every problem, plan for every possible outcome, and exert control over every situation. This can look different for each individual, but in our practices, we see this manifesting in a few common ways: constant busyness, never-ending to-do lists, and exhausting projects, all in an attempt to fix, plan, and control all of the variables in our lives.

Of course, the desire to fix, plan, and control isn't always a bad thing. As humans, we have a basic biological need for control. Research indicates our emotional and physical health, and our very survival, are dependent on our perception of choice and our ability to exert control over our environment.[36] As adults, we are faced with a need to fix issues and solve problems on a daily, hourly, and moment-by-moment basis, and we all need to use a certain degree of planning to make sure we get where we need to go.

Fixing, planning, and controlling are basic life skills. We need them to function. It's when we begin *over*-functioning as a way to avoid connecting with ourselves and others that we get into trouble. To make matters worse, those of us who are prone to over-functioning get reinforced for our efforts all over the place. Take Isabel, our thirty-something friend from chapter one. She feels great when her husband tells her, "I couldn't do this without you" at the end of a perfectly executed, double-booked Saturday. Or Alyssa, who feels validated for her hard work when her friends say, "I don't know how you do it" after she works through the weekend to meet a deadline. Or Maria, who bursts with pride when her boss compliments her for being so on top of things that he'd be lost without her.

While positive feedback can feel great, it can also keep us trapped in our desire to fix, plan, and control every aspect of our lives and the lives of those around us. This is compounded by the patriarchal assumption that it is our role, as women, to fix, plan, and control the bulk of household tasks and carry the cognitive load within the family. We may find purpose and appreciation in our roles, but it is incredibly difficult to stay connected to who we are as individuals when we feel like we have no choice but to manage all the fixing, planning, and controlling for the family.

We over-function because we don't trust the people in our lives to help us and because we've picked up on the insidious societal messaging about our responsibility as women to "do it all." In response, we feel a constant urgency or rigidity that makes it difficult to stay present, open, and flexible. Isabel often finds herself creating a "flow chart" of sorts for every possible outcome or issue that could come her way. *What if the five-year-old gets the stomach bug that the eight-year-old had last week? He'll be devastated if he can't go to his kindergarten bike rodeo. Oh, no! What if he has to stay home sick? I can't leave him home by himself, but I've put so much time and effort into organizing that event. I've got to be there. I'll have to ask George if he can be on tap to work from home next Friday just in case.* All of the coordinating and managing of schedules and tasks makes it hard for Isabel to stay connected in her own life.

When our cognitive space is overloaded with logistics, there's not much room for our feelings. Fixing, planning, and controlling serve to distract us from our difficult emotions. For example, the summer after Maria's son graduated from high school, she became fixated on setting up his dorm room. She spent her days consumed with college mom blogs, YouTube videos of move-in days, and dorm room Pinterest boards. She looked up all the best organizational systems, found the most popular shower caddy, and bought the highest rated small appliances for her son's new home. She dedicated her free time to shopping, researching, and organizing—anything to keep her in constant motion in the hopes that she might outrun her own feelings about becoming an empty nester.

The desire to fix, plan, and control really comes back to a lack of trust. For example, if Isabel could trust the version of herself that shows up next Friday to deal with whatever stomach bug, childcare need, or unpredictable chaos that day has in store, she could fix, plan, and control less. If Maria could trust herself to sit with discomfort, she wouldn't have to busy herself with logistics and short-circuit uncomfortable feelings about her son leaving home. However, since many of us don't trust ourselves to handle whatever comes our way in real time, we get caught up in pre-fixing potential problems, overplanning logistics, and attempting to control all situations all the time. We beat ourselves up for failing to anticipate negative outcomes and try to figure out every detail before the next thing happens. There's always an issue to be fixed or planned, so we stay stuck in our heads.

Worrying about things being done "right" or feeling that we are the only ones who can do something correctly makes it hard to trust other people and interferes with our ability to ask for help and delegate appropriately. It's impossible to stay connected to ourselves when we're always in motion, which makes the desire to fix, plan, and control a huge driver of self-abandonment.

So, how do we fix this lack of trust and its negative impact on our relationship with ourselves? By tuning back into ourselves and believing in our own ability to figure out and handle what comes up as it happens. By trusting our IGS. And how do we do this for others? By trusting them to help carry the load and considering that everything could (and probably will) be fine even if we don't have total control over and can't perfectly orchestrate the outcome. In other words, rather than trying to exert control, we can treat ourselves and others with care and compassion instead.

Self-Doubt

One thing we see consistently with clients who have abandoned themselves is an underlying sense of self-doubt. They constantly question themselves and often become paralyzed when making decisions, big and small. Making space for who they might be and what they might dare to do with their lives is constantly overshadowed with "what-ifs" and fears of the unknown. Is a little bit of self-doubt normal? Sure. But when you constantly question your capabilities and even who you are, self-doubt can really get in your way.

Self-doubt is a state of uncertainty in which you lack faith or confidence in yourself. It often takes the form of internal questioning: *Did I make the right decision getting bangs? Should I eat that piece of cake? Does my boss think I'm competent? Did I prepare my teen enough for college?* This anxious type of questioning, whether around small and inconsequential things or big and meaningful things, can feel endless and can easily spiral out of control.

It is a vicious cycle: The more we doubt ourselves, the harder it is to connect with ourselves, and the more disconnected we are from ourselves, the greater our self-doubt.

When we doubt ourselves, it negatively affects us in all kinds of ways, but let's start with how it causes us to downplay our accomplishments. For example, Alyssa recently completed a major project at work, resulting in a huge boost in sales for the quarter. As she presented her results to upper management, she found herself automatically brushing off any compliments she received for her hard work. "It wasn't a big deal," she said multiple times when people asked about her strategy. But it *was* a big deal. She had put a massive amount of time and effort into the project, and her strategy was innovative and effective. It wasn't that Alyssa was trying to be humble. Rather, her self-doubt had taken over. She worried her bosses were praising her just to be nice, and she further dismissed the compliments because she convinced herself that anyone else in her shoes could have done the same thing.

When was the last time you expressed pride about something *you* did? How many times have you used the words *only* or *kind of* in front of a behavior to downplay its significance? "I only ran six miles." "I only got my master's degree." "I kind of did okay in that interview." "I kind of helped coordinate the bake sale." Women are socialized to minimize and qualify their accomplishments but expected to express confidence and pride in others.

On the flip side, how many times do you express pride in your kids or your partner as compared to yourself? Big difference, right?

Research has shown that women have an especially difficult time with self-promotion, often due to fear of backlash from others.[37] One study even found that this gender gap in self-promotion begins as early as the sixth grade![38] In her book *On Our Best Behavior*, author Elise Loehnen describes women's seemingly universal difficulty with pride and shares her own struggles expressing pride in herself: "When I say I'm proud of myself I almost choke in embarrassment. I'm much more comfortable caveating, minimizing" (p. 91).[39]

Self-doubt can lead to chronic approval-seeking from others. After all, if we don't have faith in ourselves, it's human nature to look to our EGS and try to find someone else to fill that void. This can result in difficulty listening to our own IGS, including our wants and needs. When we value the opinions of others over our own intuition, we send ourselves the message that we cannot trust ourselves.

Furthermore, self-doubt can lead to difficulty making decisions. Oftentimes, we get caught in the belief that we need to make the "right" decision, rather than the most workable or effective one. We believe that there is one correct decision and get lost trying to select the best option. Self-doubt leaves us stuck in our heads, swirling round and round in rumination.

Lastly, self-doubt oftentimes underlies unhelpful comparisons. It's natural for all of us to seek out feedback about our skills, abilities, and performance. We all compare ourselves to others to see how we measure up. In the best of circumstances, we use this "research" to increase our motivation for self-improvement. But in the worst of circumstances, frequent social comparisons can increase feelings of anxiety, disappointment, guilt, and self-doubt.

Nowhere is this more prominent than the landscape of social media. All it takes is one visit to Instagram to get a barrage of other people doing things "better" than you, from packing school lunches to decorating their homes to taking luxury vacations. How do you feel when you engage in this type of social comparison? Our guess is that your self-doubt skyrockets.

The problem with all forms of self-abandonment (getting stuck in your head; numbing; seeking constant self-improvement; and willfully disengaging) and the core issues underlying self-abandonment (self-judgment; fear of discomfort; the desire to fix, plan, and control; and self-doubt) is they lead to disconnection from ourselves and others, causing pervasive loneliness and distance from what truly matters most to us.

Instead, we want you to enjoy the full-bodied experience of tuning inward. We want you to truly feel what you're feeling, without judgment or unnecessary suffering. We want you to be able to identify and effectively respond to your wants and needs so you can have more satisfying relationships with others.

So, how are we going to continue to help you get there? In a word: connection. And connection starts with you. In the next section, we'll talk about some helpful mindsets to keep you connected to yourself.

Helpful Mindsets

It was one of those weeks. From intense work deadlines to planning and hosting her mother's eightieth birthday party, Maria felt frantic and exhausted. She found herself distracted, disconnected, and irritable. She was angry with her siblings for not offering to help with their mom's party, and she snapped when her sister asked if she was going to make their mom's favorite chocolate cake. *Of course she was going to make Mom's favorite cake! Just like she was going to do everything else.* As Maria was making the cake, she realized she was out of eggs, and as she jumped in her car to head to the store, she received a message from her boss, criticizing several aspects of a brief she'd submitted earlier that day. Maria's brain leaped into an anxious spiral, and she started planning how she was going to get everything done, including fixing the flawed brief. She was on autopilot, and before she knew it, she was ordering tacos from the drive-thru down the street.

Sound familiar? So many of us can relate to Maria, day in and day out.

But here is where all the work that Maria has done came in to help her stay connected, rather than numb out or get stuck in her head. Something clicked when she got her to-go order, and she realized that she was falling into old habits. She caught herself spiraling, and instead of getting sucked into and consumed by the thoughts and feelings, she simply parked her car and took a moment to observe what was happening inside her.

She started by getting curious. *What's going on for me right now? How am I feeling? What's happening in my body? What truth am I stuffing down? What do I really want or need?* She asked herself these questions slowly, one by one, making space for whatever response might float to the surface as she was tuning in. She noticed overwhelm, resentment, and anger, and she had the feeling she was being taken advantage of. She felt devastated as a result of her boss's critical feedback and admitted that she was terrified he might think less of her. She felt pressure in her head, like it was going to explode, and her breathing was rapid. She also recognized a few truths:

- Although she felt an urgency to "fix" the brief that night, she didn't have the capacity for a late-night work session.
- She wanted help from her siblings with her mom, but asking for help felt uncomfortable. She didn't trust that her siblings would follow through "correctly," and a part of her felt like she should be able to manage on her own.

Once Maria took the time to realize what she was feeling, she was able to recognize all the judgments that were weighing her down in this stressful moment. She was judging herself for picking up tacos instead of cooking a homemade meal. She was judging herself as incompetent for not getting a perfect work review. She was judging her siblings for not doing their share of the work for their mother.

However, instead of getting swept into these judgments, she simply observed them, again drawing on curiosity. *Oh, wow, look at all these judgments.* She was also able to remind herself, *Somehow, I've come to equate not being able to do it all with being lazy. I'm not sure that's a fair or accurate comparison.* She allowed herself to say, *I'm proud of myself for catching the numbing and disconnection. I was really overwhelmed, and it makes sense I'd reach for comfort food like tacos. And I'm actually hungry, so a taco is a great choice to both nourish myself and get some mindful comfort.*

This is the beauty of tuning in and connecting to ourselves. When Maria shifted out of her automatic response of overthinking and numbing, she was able to tap into openness and willingness. She was open to looking inward and willing to shift into *responding* rather than *reacting*. Maria also tapped into openness and willingness when working with her discomfort about getting negative feedback from her boss. She started by taking a more open physical stance: She lowered her shoulders away from her ears, opened her palms, and relaxed her face. She was aware that she didn't like getting negative feedback on the brief, but she was willing to sit down with the document to see if there was a kernel of truth to what her boss was saying and possibly rework the brief based on that.

Let's take a closer look at the helpful mindsets Maria put into practice: curiosity, nonjudgment, and openness and willingness.

Curiosity

Getting curious is about observing your internal experience and learning new information, not about judging your experience or coming up with the "right" answer. Three simple questions for practicing curiosity are:

- What stories am I telling myself?
- What sensations am I noticing in my body?
- What emotions am I feeling?

Nonjudgment

Being nonjudgmental means taking the focus off the good/bad, approve/disapprove dichotomous mindset. It's about describing the facts of the situation and noticing the consequences so that you can make wise choices on how to move forward. So instead of telling yourself, *I'm such a lazy slob for not exercising today*, you could simply say, *I didn't exercise today*. If you wanted to be more descriptive about the situation, you could even say, *I didn't exercise today because I did not get enough rest last night. Movement helps me feel better physically and emotionally, so I will ensure I get a good night's rest so I can move tomorrow.*

Openness and Willingness

Openness and willingness help you become unstuck by providing you with feedback about your blind spots. This allows you to respond to unexpected or difficult situations in helpful and effective ways. A couple of clues for when openness and willingness might be really helpful: when you are in a new situation, are being challenged or criticized in some way, or feel invalidated. You can also foster openness and willingness in your physical body. You can notice the degree of constriction (tension, tightness, closedness, or scarcity) versus the degrees of openness (space, breathing room, freedom, or abundance) in your body. This is a great variable to tune in to in your daily life: *Where in my body do I feel any tightness or constriction? How can I open up or loosen?*

Tuning In: Let It All Belong

As we've discussed, we often abandon ourselves because sitting with our emotions is uncomfortable and hard. We engage in all kinds of acrobatics to try not to feel our feelings: We ignore, distract, avoid, disconnect, run away from (sometimes quite literally), suppress, or get caught in efforts to fix, plan, or control. Often, we sidestep our emotions without even knowing that's what we're doing. For many of us, these actions are fast, automatic, and unconscious.

You already know that short-circuiting emotions can be problematic for coping and overall well-being, but it bears going a little deeper here. Research shows that suppressing our emotions doesn't actually help us alter unwanted emotions. (In fact, they're still there and more likely to wreak havoc the further we stuff them down!)[40] In addition, stuffing down our emotions prevents us from enjoying any *wanted* emotions too. Repressing our feelings decreases positive emotions, activates our sympathetic nervous system (the part of our biology associated with the fight, flight, or freeze response), depletes our cognitive resources, and interferes with our capacity to connect with others.

Additionally, stuffing down our emotions increases the risk of mental health issues, such as depression, anxiety, and eating disorders.[41, 42] It can also lead these emotions to erupt into a major emotional meltdown (or even mini temper tantrum) or to come out sideways through judgmental or passive-aggressive behavior. In other words, ignoring our emotions and stuffing them down can later backfire.

There are many benefits to instead making space for our emotions. As annoying as they might feel at times, we really do need our feelings. We have emotions for a reason, and most of the time, they're just trying to help us. For instance, if you feel scared when walking alone through a seedy part of town at night, this fear might be nudging you to get the heck out of there! Or if you feel angry when your partner spends your date night on his phone watching college football, your anger might be communicating that you need to set a boundary.

Of course, there are times when our emotions can go haywire. For example, after a trying day at work, we might overreact by screaming at our child when they spill milk on the floor. Or we might burst into tears when we receive some reasonable, constructive criticism from a boss. When our emotions are disproportionate to the situation, or even totally disconnected from the reality of what's going on, or when we can't identify a reason for why we're feeling a certain way, it might be a clue that we need extra support from a licensed mental health professional (via therapy or medication). Tuning in practices can still be super helpful in such moments, *and* sometimes we need more.

We get it, this is hard work. But the rewards are huge. Understanding our emotions can change our experience of them. When we work with our feelings rather than fighting, judging, avoiding, or overidentifying with them, all those things we are tasked with doing and accomplishing each day tend to go more smoothly. We're better able to regulate our emotions. We can *respond* rather than react.

Most importantly, working *with* instead of *against* our emotions helps us connect with ourselves, tune in to our wants and needs, and make wise and honest decisions in response. For example, if you can identify that you're feeling lonely, you can reach out to a friend to connect. If you realize you're feeling resentful about doing your teenagers' laundry each week, you can plan to turn over this task to them. If you're feeling unmotivated in your career, you can make thoughtful progress toward changing your situation.

So how, exactly, do you let all your emotions belong? First, you tune in. Recognize how you're feeling, naming each emotion clearly. (If you need help naming your feelings, refer to the feelings list in the appendix.) And then you just let your feelings be. That's it.

Tips for Letting It All Belong

As you continue to practice tuning in to and naming your emotions, keep these things in mind:

- **Think of emotions like waves on a beach.** They roll in, and they roll out. You don't have to make the waves come and go; they just exist. Sometimes, the waves are smooth and quiet; other times, they crash loudly upon the shore. No one wave and no one feeling lasts forever. They come in, they crest, and then they leave.
- **Deliberately welcome your emotions.** When you notice a specific emotion, welcome it directly: *Hi, Anxiety, we're tuning in.* Or *Oh hello, Not-Enoughness. So glad you're joining me for the car ride. Hop on in! But keep your sticky hands off the wheel!*
- **Make friends with your emotions.** When you notice an emotion, get curious about it. Ask your emotions some questions: *Hi, Anger, what are you doing here? Envy, is there anything you want me to know? Tell me about yourself, Sadness.*

Will this feel a little silly at first? Maybe. But we promise, the more you practice and see the benefits, the more natural this will feel.

For example, before Alyssa started tuning in, she would often get caught in immense self-judgment and overwhelm. She'd start to have a negative feeling about her job and daydream about working shorter hours and doing something more fulfilling, when judgment would suddenly swoop in: *Why is this so hard for you? Everyone else manages the craziness of this job without complaining so much or getting so stressed. What's wrong with you?* In addition to judgment, fear would arise: *You'll never find another job that pays you this much. If you leave now, you'll be ruining your career.* On some level, Alyssa knew she was lonely. She didn't have much social time, and she felt hopeless about finding a romantic partner who would love her. But admitting she was lonely felt uncomfortable, so it was easier to set those feelings aside and pour herself into her work. As you can see, there was a lot Alyssa was ignoring.

When she started the practice of letting it all belong, Alyssa made space for all her feelings to exist, without judgment, explanation, or the need to fix. Instead of going through all the acrobatics to avoid her emotions, Alyssa practiced just feeling: *Gosh, I am so lonely. Wow, work is really stressful and exhausting. I'm so depleted, and truth be told, I really don't like my job or working this much. I wish I had a boyfriend, but I feel so scared to date. I worry I won't ever find anyone.* Instead of getting sucked into the judgments, she simply noticed them: *Wow, I have a lot of judgment about how I'm feeling and what I'm doing. Eek, I'm hard on myself.* She made friends with her loneliness. Her anxiety and fear. Her exhaustion. Her not-enoughness. She asked them what they wanted and needed and how she could take care of them. Instead of being hard on herself, Alyssa showed up for herself with understanding and empathy.

The same thing happened when Isabel, our thirty-something mom of three, put this into practice during a particularly painful situation with her husband. She'd been cleaning up when she stumbled across her husband's iPad. His browser was up, and she was shocked to see him logged into a pornography website. She took a closer look at their credit card statements and saw charges for hundreds of dollars to this same online site. She was irate. She was like a loaded pistol, ready to fire.

However, when she tuned inward, she noticed she needed some time and space to herself. She recognized that she was, not surprisingly, struck with a wave of anger. She felt the urge to lash out: *How dare George betray me like this? What a piece of shit!* She then noticed a quick barrage of self-judgments: *It's your fault he's looking at porn. You've been too exhausted to focus on your sex life, and let's be honest, when was the last time you got spruced up to set the mood? You've really let yourself go. What was he supposed to do?*

Instead of spiraling into despair, Isabel kept breathing deeply and continued to be curious about what else might be happening inside her. Underneath the anger, she noticed confusion and fear, doubt and uncertainty. *What does all this mean? What's going to happen to our marriage? What if this is the end?* She allowed herself to feel significant sadness and grief around the changes in their marriage since having children. When those feelings started to feel overwhelming, she reminded herself that feelings are like waves, that they would come and go and not last forever. She practiced self-compassion by wrapping her arms around herself in a hug and gently rocking back and forth as the tears streamed down her cheeks. She told herself, *Ugh. This is really hard right now.* Isabel then took some notes in her journal about how she was feeling.

When we let our feelings belong, we change our relationship with them, which, in turn, helps decrease our suffering. And we don't have to zero in on any particular feeling or let one particular emotion take over. We often use the analogy of telescoping out: Let the one feeling belong and make space to see what else is present. We might ask ourselves, *What else is there? Can I make space for that too? Can I make space for it all to belong?*

Over time, we realize we can tolerate uncomfortable feelings and experiences without rushing to avoid, figure out, fix, or disconnect. Again, no one is asking you to get rid of your emotions. The goal is not to change your emotions. The goal is to simply *feel* them. This simple act helps you stay present with and for yourself and in relationship with others. And the best part is that when you're able to stay present and connected, especially when life throws you curveballs, you don't abandon yourself.

Tuning In: Self-Compassion—the Antidote to Self-Judgment

Many of us automatically default to self-judgment throughout our lives, even when we haven't made a "mistake" or failed in some way. We simply treat ourselves harshly at all times. And when we have messed up, giving ourselves grace can be even harder. It feels easier, and more socially acceptable, to get caught up in self-criticism and to punish ourselves for our shortcomings. We're so busy treating ourselves horribly that we don't make room to *feel* the pain. And ironically, judging ourselves only leads to more pain.

Self-compassion is the balm in such moments, whether or not we're technically to blame for whatever happened in the first place. In other words, self-compassion is the antidote to self-judgment.[43]

You'll recall from chapter two that self-compassion is showing up for yourself and treating yourself like you would a dear friend, especially when you're having a hard time. It's being kind to yourself. It's recognizing that you're not alone in your suffering. If self-compassion kind of sounds like magic, that's because it really can be. Here's an example of how self-compassion showed up and saved the day for Isabel.

Isabel was feeling great when she picked up her ten-year-old daughter, Olivia, from school one Tuesday afternoon. However, she could tell something was wrong when her daughter climbed into the back of the car and angrily slammed down her backpack. "Mom," she said with tears in her eyes, "How come you weren't at my field trip today?"

Isabel felt her blood fall to her feet. The field trip. The one she'd promised Olivia she would chaperone, the last one of the school year, the last one before Olivia went off to middle school.

"Oh, Olivia," Isabel said, trying to think of an excuse as to why she didn't show up. But Olivia pulled her knees into her chest and wordlessly stared out the window. There was nothing Isabel could do to take away her daughter's hurt feelings, and she knew it.

As soon as they arrived home, Isabel fled to her bathroom and burst into tears.

She spiraled quickly, chronicling all the ways she'd failed as a mom, berating herself for all her imperfections. She was not as present, patient, or involved as she "should" have been. Then, she moved quickly into catastrophizing the future: *I am the worst mom ever. I'm never going to be able to make this up to her, am I? There's nothing I can do to turn back the hands of time.*

Thankfully, as her head was swirling, Isabel remembered the messages we've talked about in this book. She told herself, *Take a breath, Isabel. You're not getting anywhere or making any decisions without starting with self-compassion.*

After a few long moments of sitting with her pain, sadness, and embarrassment, she found herself quietly reminding herself: *Wow, this is really hard. I'm so disappointed in myself. I feel sad for Olivia. I feel sad for myself. I feel regret and shame. I'm so afraid of losing my daughter's trust. That's a lot to hold. I've got you, Isabel. I'm right here with you.*

The swirling feelings of panic and shame subsided. She felt a quiet peace descend upon her.

And Isabel finally understood—truly, in the depths of her soul, *understood.*

She was not going to waste a single moment of time being overly critical and angry at herself. What was done was done. She told herself that moving forward, she would do better, and she said this with genuine care, rather than harsh judgment. This mistake was painful, but it was going to be okay. She and Olivia would be okay.

This is the gift of self-compassion.

We can go toe-to-toe with our anxiety all day long, going round and round in an endless, never-ending battle. We can collapse in the pit of regret and self-judgment. We can try to control it all. And we can ignore, distract, avoid, or stay indefinitely busy. But there is a better way.

We can let it *all* belong. We can show up for ourselves with compassion and kindness, even when it's hard. We can name our feelings honestly and authentically, especially when it's painful. And in doing this, we can bypass all the other conditioning we've perhaps been stuck in for decades and make room for more connection, peace, and ease in our daily lives.

Self-Compassion Practices

1. **Talk to yourself like you would a dear friend.** Ask yourself questions. Listen to your intuition. Use a warm, gentle voice. Have an open body posture.
2. **Let it all belong.** Allow yourself to feel whatever you are feeling. Avoid going to the past with regret, self-judgment, self-aggression, or rumination. Avoid going to the future with planning, problem-solving, or trying to fix. Name your present feelings.
3. **Soften into your emotions and into your body.** If compassion had a shape, it'd be soft, round, and open, rather than constricted, sharp, and closed. Whereas self-judgment feels rigid, harsh, uncomfortable, and even painful, compassion is warm, gentle, soft, comforting, and soothing. As you settle into your body, imagine rounded corners instead of rigid, hard lines. Visualize a soft place to land. When we're soft and open, we feel more connected and alive.

4. **Practice loving-kindness.** Create your own loving-kindness phrases. Some examples include:
    - *May I be free of suffering.*
    - *May I be filled with peace and ease.*
    - *May I be fully present.*
    - *May I live with abundant joy.*
    - *May I be filled with compassion for myself and others.*
    - *May I know I'm already enough.*
    - *May I listen to and trust myself.*

You can tailor these phrases to whatever you need in the moment. And you can also offer loving-kindness to others, for example: *May all beings be free from suffering.*

Make no mistake about it: Your harsh, self-critical voice—your intense and often automatic and unconscious self-judgments—are having a negative impact on your well-being. Tuning in and tapping into self-compassion turns the whole system on its head. With practice, you will become very skilled at "catching" your self-judgments before they take hold. We have even seen women make a game out of counting how many judgments flit across their minds on any given day! The game of "catching" judgments brings levity and humor into the experience, meaning that with some practice, you can good-naturedly roll your eyes at subconscious judgments instead of taking them so seriously.

If you would describe yourself as busy, frantic, critical, rigid, needing to be right, or fiercely independent, practicing self-compassion can help you round the corners of these sharp edges, so to speak. Start by unclenching your fists, relaxing your brow, letting your mouth turn upward into a half smile, and expanding open across your chest and shoulders. Imagine all your insides softening, curling, and curving. As you inhale, imagine gathering up the stress, tension, and feelings of urgency in your body and then releasing them—physically breathing them out—as you exhale.

Watch how this practice impacts your day-to-day behaviors. You might find that some of those activities that felt like chores—your exercise routine, your social schedule—feel more manageable, lighter, and even enjoyable. You will be quite literally setting the stage for embodying curiosity, openness, and willingness.

We have a dear teacher and fellow mental health professional, Taylor White Moffitt, who says, "Self-compassion delivers everything that self-improvement promises." Take a moment to let that sink in. Ultimately, all our efforts toward self-improvement are focused on the goal of feeling like we're enough. Like we're okay, acceptable, lovable, worthy, and not alone. The practice of self-compassion offers all these results.

Do Try This at Home

#1: Catch Your Judgments

Many self-judgments can be sneaky and automatic—you're often not even aware of them! Play detective by becoming aware of your judgments and "catching" them when you notice them. The goal is to simply become more *aware* of them, which helps change your relationship with them.

#2: Create Your Own Personalized Loving-Kindness Phrases

Refer back to the self-compassion practices earlier in this chapter to help get you started. Choose or create some loving-kindness phrases that fit where you are today. Repeat these silently to yourself for a few minutes.

#3: Practice Letting It All Belong

Bring to mind a situation in your life that stirs up feelings. Practice making space for all your feelings to belong. You can welcome them and make friends with them. Greet each feeling warmly. Ask yourself, *What else might I be feeling?*

#4: Pick a Helpful Mindset to Leverage

We talked about curiosity, nonjudgment, openness, and willingness. Which of these do you need most in your life right now? What are some ways you can practice the one you need most?

Chapter 5

Connection and Belonging

So far, we've discussed the importance of staying connected to ourselves, but of course, we aren't just in relationship with ourselves. To be human is to be in relationship with others. And as we all know, relationships with others can be . . . tricky. As psychologists, the three of us know that to be truly fulfilled, we must stay connected to ourselves *and* bring our authentic selves to our relationships with the outside world. Now it's time to discuss the intersection between us, individually, and the rest of the world. It's where "me" becomes "we."

The Need for Belonging, Connection, and Community

Belonging is a basic human need and is fundamental to understanding human nature.[44] No matter if you're introverted or extroverted, as humans, we're wired for connection. Being included feels like a matter of life or death because, evolutionarily speaking, it is. We simply cannot survive on our own. We are highly motivated to stay in relationship with others, so we constantly jump through all kinds of hoops to stay connected. We experience rejection as physically painful.[45] So, we prioritize others, try to please them, and do anything within our power to avoid exclusion.

And yet, in all our desperate attempts to stay connected with others, we risk losing connection to ourselves. There is a big difference between truly belonging and simply fitting in. Where belonging is grounded in unconditional acceptance, fitting in is based on conditional approval. Fitting in with a group often requires us to sacrifice the parts of ourselves that don't fit, while true belonging requires us to stay fully connected to ourselves. In other words, we ultimately harm ourselves and stay disconnected when we abandon ourselves to fit in.

We often see women hold their friends at arm's length and fear that open and honest communication will set them up for rejection, but we find the opposite to be true. The more of the "real" you that you show to your trusted circle, the more you make way for true acceptance.

Is showing the "real" you hard, scary, and vulnerable? Of course! Telling your friends the truth when it comes to your fears, failures, and deepest concerns is about as vulnerable as it gets. What if people see that your marriage isn't perfect? What if people discover that the life you portray on social media isn't always smiles and vacations? We get it! But we also know through our work as psychologists and from our own lived experiences that when we are open and honest with each other, our friends feel more comfortable sharing real issues with us as a result. Honesty deepens friendships. The women who are most fulfilled by their social lives and the least lonely are the ones who are willing to be real and raw with the people around them.

True belonging requires us to choose our people wisely. We simply must prioritize people who feel safe and comfortable and walk away from those who don't. This can be easier said than done, but it's essential if we are looking for true, authentic connection. Stay tuned: We'll talk more about this in the pages ahead.

Authentic relationships can be difficult to find and maintain, especially in today's society. Even if we have strong relationships, it's easy to forget we *need* a village to survive. We have become independent to the point of isolation. We move so fast and frantically that we don't prioritize leisurely, in-person connections with people in our communities. We don't feel like we have time to chat with or help our neighbors, and we're so distracted by our schedules and our devices that we don't take advantage of opportunities to connect with the people around us. We feel overloaded and overburdened. We're already taking care of so much that we lose the capacity for genuine interactions with others.

As a result of our constant busyness, there's been an erosion of community, and the loneliness epidemic has had a profound impact on our mental and physical health. We may view getting together with friends as an optional fun activity, but spending time with friends is necessary! In fact, social connection matters more to our longevity than what we eat and how much we exercise, and it is the number one buffer against stress. So, we must prioritize our friendships, nurture the relationships we have, and take time to meet and bond with new people in our community.

Lots of women come to therapy because they want to make their relationships better, but as we already know from the previous chapters of this book, everything starts with us. Keep this in mind as we move through this chapter. Real connection in relationships *requires* us to be connected with ourselves first. We must be grounded in ourselves—to have access to our own feelings and intuition—to be able to authentically connect with one another. To ask for what we really want, we have to actually know what we really want. To communicate how we actually feel, we need to have access to our emotions. We must connect with who we really are before we can show our authentic selves to each other. Belonging in any relationship, whether with our significant other, our friends, or even our colleagues, *requires* us to stay connected to ourselves.

Tuning In: Leverage Your IGS

We first have to be connected to ourselves before we can really connect with others. We have to know and trust our own intuition as we're connecting in our relationships. The tuning-in practices we've covered thus far are your first step. Listening to and trusting yourself, letting it all belong, and practicing self-compassion all apply in relationships. One final aspect of tuning in, which we've alluded to in the prior chapters, involves connecting with and leveraging your intuition, your IGS.

Tuning in helps you know yourself better. It helps you answer the questions "Who am I?" and "What do I want and need?" You access these answers by tuning in to your IGS. As you learned in chapter one, this is the small, quiet, still voice within you. It's wise and centered, leading you with clarity and knowing.

If you allow yourself space and stillness, quiet and solitude, if you allow yourself to *listen* to your intuition, you're afforded clarity and a sense of peace. Not just for how you show up for yourself, but how you show up in your relationships. You've probably heard about this before, but it's hard to know what this means in practice.

First, let's start with how your intuition speaks to you. Your IGS doesn't speak in long sentences. It often communicates through a gut feeling, a felt sense of knowing, without many words at all. It creates a powerful feedback loop: The more you listen to and honor your IGS, the more you know and trust yourself, and the less likely you are to abandon yourself.

Following your inner sense of knowing sounds pretty woo-woo, and we get that. But we know from experience that getting into the habit of trusting ourselves really works. We don't have to overthink or get overwhelmed by emotions, we just *know*. For example, Alyssa had just finished a lukewarm first date, and after she got home, she received a text message from the potential suitor asking if she wanted to go out again the next week. She took a quick moment to tune in, closing her eyes and placing her hands over her heart. She was struck with a quick and loud

"No!" Without having to analyze or question this answer, she responded that she would pass. Done. She didn't need to think twice.

Similarly, Isabel was able to connect with her IGS to gain wisdom about what was happening in her life and what she needed to do about it. Tuning in gave her the confidence to talk to George about his pornography use and address the real elephant in the room: the cracks that had formed in their marriage, which she desperately wanted to fix. In addition, when tapping into her IGS, she had a sense that her marriage would benefit from a regular, weekly date night, which meant investing in childcare, and in making that important discovery, she admitted she felt ready and excited to go back to work. She missed the creative, career-oriented part of herself and wanted to invest in something that was hers. She especially wanted to create a life of her own as her kids became more independent and needed her less.

See what we mean? The more you make space to listen to what you truly want and need, the more you can trust yourself to make it happen.

There are two simple practices to help connect with your IGS. The first is to let your breath guide you to your intuition, which you've already been practicing. Take a few moments to just breathe into your inner wisdom. If you need a mantra to help anchor your attention, here are some options: "be still," "listen deeply" or "stay connected." You don't need to force anything. Just be open and curious. The second practice is to simply ask yourself, *What does my IGS say?*

Whether it's a decision you're trying to make, a problem you're trying to solve, or even just a feeling you're trying to name, tuning in reveals your intuition, your gut feeling, your inner wisdom. Once you connect with your IGS, you can use this wisdom to guide and direct you. As a warning, you're not always going to get a clear answer of what to do. Sometimes, your intuition will say, *I don't know what the next step is yet. I don't know what all the answers are. Here's what I know at this moment in time.* That is okay. The point is to practice listening to your IGS and give yourself the opportunity to connect with what your inner wisdom tells you to do.

We can't stress this enough: Be gentle and patient with yourself. Many people feel disconnected from their IGS when they first try to access it. Don't worry—we all have an IGS. She is there inside you. Sometimes, it takes a little time to reconnect. Some days and moments will be easier than others. Keep listening. You'll hear her soon.

Communication Skills

Tapping into your inner knowing is more than a practice that keeps you connected to yourself. It can also be extremely valuable when navigating life—including difficult situations—with the people you love. The next sections will help you fine-tune the communication skills you will need when prioritizing your IGS.

Speak Truth

A few weeks after Ruby's son, Marcus, had lost his job and she helped him pay some of his bills and downsize into a smaller apartment, she received her credit card statement in the mail. She opened the envelope and noticed there were hundreds of dollars in charges from Amazon for items she didn't purchase: cologne, a gaming console, and men's clothing, to name a few. She must have let out an audible gasp, because her partner, Paul, who was seated on the couch reading, looked up and asked what was wrong.

Ruby's anxiety kicked into high gear. She knew who had purchased those items on her account, and she also knew how Paul felt about Marcus: He was a grown man who needed to get his act together and could use some "tough love."

Ruby was well-versed in the tuning-in exercises we've covered in this book, so she excused herself from the living room and headed to her bedroom to be alone and steady herself. Ruby knew that Marcus had gone too far and that she needed to do something about it. She wanted to handle this situation from a place of being grounded in her own intuition and knowing. Ruby needed to take a moment and listen to what her gut was telling her about the next steps, to get clear on what truth needed to be spoken.

When couples and families come to us for therapy, they are usually looking for ways to improve communication. We spend a lot of time encouraging our clients to tell the truth about their experiences, feelings, wants, or needs. It's one thing to do this in our own heads. But telling the truth to others, especially those we love, can feel incredibly anxiety-provoking, awkward, or even painful. We often swallow our words so as not to offend or upset anyone. Our desire to be polite or keep the peace might lead us to say what we believe others want to hear. So, yes, on the outside, we are meeting everyone's expectations. But on the inside, we are moving further and further away from our authentic selves.

While your intentions might be good, not speaking truth to others, especially when it's hard, is very costly. It taxes your mind and body. Failing to say what you mean or choosing to stay silent when you feel compelled to speak up activates your fight, flight, or freeze response. Your body doesn't like this one bit. You are likely to experience more tension, poorer sleep, worsened anxiety and mood, and more relationship difficulties.[46] On the other hand, when you speak truth, your brain is calm, cool, and collected. Your nervous system settles. Yes, even when it's hard. Even when it's awkward. Even when it's scary.

The good news is that we feel most connected to ourselves and others when truth is being spoken. Biting our tongues might feel like a good idea in the short run, but in the long run, it doesn't feel good to hide who we are. Over time, not speaking truth diminishes our self-respect and how we feel about ourselves in general. It's also incredibly hard to connect when we're not honest with others. We may be able to stuff down uncomfortable truths for a while, but the truth inevitably comes out, whether accidentally, in frustration or sarcasm, or in a rage-filled eruption of volcanic proportions.

Let's return to our friend Ruby. When she took some time to tune in and listen to her intuition, she knew she was stuck between a proverbial rock and a hard place. She could feel butterflies in her stomach, an internal shakiness, and a heaviness in her chest. She didn't want to be the sort of partner who wasn't honest and transparent. She also didn't want Paul to be angry with Marcus, nor did she want Paul to intervene on her behalf. This was going to be a tough conversation with both Paul and her son, and she knew that no matter what she said, someone would be unhappy. Rather than shoving that truth away, Ruby allowed herself to feel how powerless she felt in that moment: *Both Paul and Marcus are likely going to be unhappy, and I can't control that.*

Ruby knew that the first step in dealing with this complicated situation was to speak her truth. And to speak her truth, she first had to know her own truth. That is the same for all of us. Sometimes, we're so disconnected from ourselves that we don't even know what we think, feel, or need. That's when we connect with our IGS. When something important needs to be said, we can usually *feel* it deep down in our gut.

Below are examples of hard and vulnerable truths that we often rush past because they can feel so painful. Saying hard things requires practice. Take a moment to read each statement. Do so slowly, taking a deep breath after each one. Pay attention to what happens in your body:

- *I don't know what to do.*
- *I'm so lonely.*
- *I can't fix it.*
- *This is so incredibly hard.*
- *I'm not perfect.*
- *I feel heartbroken.*

Speaking truth requires vulnerability, which we will cover in more detail in the next section. Until then, it's important to note that when you speak truth, you're taking a risk. And we get it—taking risks can be scary, to say the least. So, if you know a difficult truth needs to be spoken, how do you go about speaking it?

Here are a few tips to help you on your truth-telling journey:

1. **Pay attention to what you feel in your body.** When you're trying to decide whether there's a truth that needs to be spoken, use your skills of tuning inward. Slow down, let your emotions belong, practice self-compassion, and ask yourself what you want and need. Discern what needs to be said.
2. **Practice by starting small and sharing preferences.** When your friend asks, "Where do you want to go to dinner?" are you inclined to say, "Anywhere is fine," or are you more likely to say, "I've had a lot of Mexican food lately, but Greek food sounds amazing"? So many of us prioritize being agreeable, flexible, or "nice" over being honest, clear, and kind. Doing this in small ways will make it easier when you need to be honest about more consequential things in your life.
3. **Be as clear as possible.** Leave out qualifiers such as "sort of" and "kind of." Instead use direct and clear wording. As Brené Brown, an expert and researcher on shame and vulnerability, writes in her book *Dare to Lead*, "Clear is kind. Unclear is unkind" (p. 48).[47] No one around you is a mind reader, and it's not fair for you to assume they are. When we're clear, we leave less room for misinterpretation (and we're more likely to get our needs met!).
4. **Speak with love, empathy, and compassion.** Our society has very few role models for speaking truth well, and it can feel incredibly overwhelming to speak truth, especially hard truths. It is possible to deliver hard truths with compassion—with clarity, honesty, and kindness. However, even when we operate with good and kind intentions and do our best in communicating, people might still

experience hurt feelings in response to something we say or do. We can't control that and that's okay.

Ruby continued taking slow, deep breaths with her hands on her chest, allowing her feelings of powerlessness, anxiety, and sadness to come and slowly fade. She took a final deep inhale and exhale, stood up, and returned to the living room courageously. "Paul, I have something to say, and it's incredibly hard to share this with you. There are unexpected Amazon charges on my credit card, and I believe they are from Marcus. I know you're worried about Marcus taking advantage of me, and I love how much you care for me. His behavior is inappropriate. I'm not sure what my next plan of action is, but I will be handling the communication with Marcus that this is not okay."

Paul agreed with her wholeheartedly, Marcus fixed the errors of his ways, and they lived happily ever after.

We're kidding! Of course, that's not what happened. Telling *your* truth doesn't always mean that everyone is going to accept it as *their* truth. It's highly likely that Paul will push back, roll his eyes, and be frustrated with Ruby for not nipping this situation in the bud earlier. Marcus will likely deflect, defend, and justify his purchases with his mother. The relationships between both men in Ruby's life might get worse before they get better, and that is okay. The point of having the courage and integrity to speak your truth isn't to have everyone agree with you or to fix things immediately. Complex situations might require time and patience. Speaking truth is powerful and transformative, but also hard and uncomfortable. We must be brave and practice holding our discomfort and ourselves with as much compassion and care as we can muster.

Be Vulnerable

There are no two ways around it—being vulnerable is scary. It doesn't matter your age, your gender, or even how much practice you have, being vulnerable requires opening yourself up to potential judgment and letting people in on what might be perceived as your weaknesses or flaws. Being vulnerable comes with significant risk. But we'd argue it's a risk worth taking.

Vulnerability is vital to connection and well-being. Brené Brown says that "to live with courage, purpose, and connection—to be the person whom we long to be—we must again be vulnerable. We must take off the armor, put down the weapons, show up, and let ourselves be seen" (p. 112).[48] Authentic connection with others requires us to drop our perfect personas, show our flaws, and be real.

Let's go back to our example of Isabel, who was going through a rough patch in her marriage. She felt hurt, betrayed, and angry about George's pornography use. They'd started to have some hard conversations as a couple, but these didn't always go very well, as they disagreed about whether or not pornography was a big deal. They were working on it, but Isabel went back and forth between feeling like they were making slow progress to being totally discouraged that they would ever come to a resolution.

For the first few weeks of therapy, Isabel didn't share anything about what was going on in her marriage with her closest friends. She felt ashamed, and though she knew her friends loved her, she worried they would think less of both her and George. After a month of keeping things inside, Isabel was feeling so lonely and isolated that she decided she needed to be vulnerable and open up to her friends over lunch.

The days leading up to lunch were tense. Isabel worried her friends would blame her for being naive, judge her for the way she handled the situation, or try to talk her into leaving her marriage right away. She was terrified there would be awkward silences or that her friends would look at her with pity. The more Isabel rehearsed the conversation in her head, the worse it became. But she was learning that if she wanted to have deep connections with her friends, she needed to make space for the hard truth. Her marriage was in trouble, and she was struggling.

Thankfully, Isabel received none of those feared responses. Her friends listened well and responded with empathy and compassion. In fact, one of her friends shared that her brother had a similar problem with pornography, and she knew from watching his struggles how painful this could be. Isabel felt huge relief in not having to carry this burden alone, and while her marital problems weren't solved over lunch, she left smiling because she knew that her friends loved her and were there to support her, no matter what. She felt great relief to not be alone in this.

Vulnerability is the glue that connects us both to ourselves and others, a vital component in coming back to the self that you may have abandoned years before. When you are vulnerable, you allow yourself to be seen, really seen. This helps build intimacy and trust, which is a two-way street. The more you practice showing up openly and authentically to others, the more they will do the same for you. Problems will get solved more easily. Shame will be reduced. And connections will be deeper and more long-lasting.

The ironic thing about vulnerability is that being truly seen by others is simultaneously one of our greatest desires and greatest fears. We're afraid we aren't enough, which causes us to hide, pretend, hustle, or overachieve to either avoid being seen altogether or to compensate for our perceived inadequacies. We're afraid that the messy, imperfect parts of ourselves are qualities we should be embarrassed about. But do you want to know the truth? Showing up and receiving love and belonging in all our messy imperfections is the exact thing that sets us free.

If you're still not convinced that you have the courage to be truly vulnerable and honest with the most important people in your life, think about it this way: How do you feel when your friends and family are vulnerable with you? Do you shame them and wish they didn't share so much of themselves with you? Of course not! In fact, you probably feel honored they've chosen to trust you and see them as courageous for having shared. We're guessing you also feel closer to them and like them more. Your relationship likely has grown as a result of these hard conversations.

The same logic applies when *you're* the one being vulnerable with others. Instead of seeing you as weak and liking you less, people will likely feel honored you've chosen to confide in them, and you'll end up being more connected. This is why the *practice* of vulnerability is so important. You must push through the experience of being vulnerable—of tolerating the discomfort and getting to the other side—to see the benefits and to really *feel and internalize* that being vulnerable is often worth it.

We wish we could guarantee that you'll always enjoy a positive outcome when you choose to be vulnerable. Often, it goes well and, ideally, your vulnerability is met with love, support, and understanding. But sometimes, despite your best efforts, people will disappoint you.

To increase the possibility of things going well, you need to practice wise discernment and set boundaries around your vulnerability. Part of this protects others—you don't want to dump all your life traumas on someone you just met! But wise discernment also protects *you*. We suggest starting with small acts of vulnerability as you build trust with someone, and become more vulnerable over time if the person responds well. If someone does not respond well—for example, they gossip about your struggles to others, shame you, exhibit judgment, or are insensitive—then perhaps what you learn is to refrain from being as vulnerable *with that specific person.*

You can expect vulnerability to be accompanied by a side of discomfort. And it's not just the moment of vulnerability that's uncomfortable, it's the aftermath. We call this a "vulnerability hangover": where we end up feeling tender and sensitive after opening up to others. This hangover is often accompanied by overthinking, replaying, and overanalyzing, and we tend to feel anxious, exhausted, distracted, and insecure. So, we avoid being vulnerable to protect ourselves, both from others' responses and from our own discomfort.

However, and we can't repeat this enough: Learning to tolerate the discomfort of being vulnerable is essential.

The good news is that you've already learned our number one tool for tolerating discomfort: our old friend, self-compassion. The practice of self-compassion allows us to stay connected to ourselves and give ourselves patience and grace while navigating difficult interactions with others. Feel free to reference back to chapters two and four for a refresher on self-compassion tools and practices.

Take Responsibility and Make Repairs

Being vulnerable and speaking the truth are important components of effective communication, but they are only the beginning when it comes to maintaining authentic relationships. Another key ingredient to effective communication is to take responsibility for ourselves, for our actions, and for our lives.

This can be hard to do, especially if our interactions with others reveal that we are at fault or need to make a change. No one likes to be at fault! No one likes to make mistakes! In such moments, it's much easier to pin the blame on external circumstances or someone else. But taking responsibility for our actions and their consequences, both intended and unintended, is an important part of staying connected to both ourselves and others. We won't always get everything right, despite our best efforts. One of the main goals of all the work you've been doing is to be okay with the fact that not everything is going to work out exactly the way you intended.

So, how do we practice taking responsibility? First, we look for our "pieces"—for the parts of the situation that we're responsible for—which requires self-reflection. Yes, we are back to the practice of tuning in! It comes up everywhere! Once we find our pieces, we take steps to make things right, which we psychologists call *making repair*. We address the issue at hand. We own up to our mistakes. This often means saying, "My bad" or "My fault" or "That's on me." Sometimes, we also need to apologize, especially if we hurt someone or dropped the ball. Owning up to our mistakes is a powerful and healing practice. It helps us feel like better human beings, and it facilitates connection and closeness in relationships.

Here's an example of how this can work in real life. Alyssa was on a committee at work that was responsible for planning the company's migration to a new software system. She was working with two other colleagues, neither of whom were pulling their weight. It would have been easy to keep her mouth shut at work and just complain to her friends and family about how frustrated and resentful she felt. Instead, she decided to address the issue directly and have a conversation about how she felt and what she would like to be different moving forward. She knew this required speaking truth and being vulnerable, and she knew it had to be done.

At the next committee meeting, Alyssa took a deep breath and worked up the courage to say, "Hey, I'm feeling a little frustrated about the division of labor, and I could really use some more specific help in a few key areas of this migration. How can we divide things up in a more equitable manner?"

Alyssa was ready for her colleagues to defend themselves and point out all the ways they had done work that she wasn't acknowledging. Instead, they admitted they had allowed much of the project to slide. One of her colleagues revealed that she had been dealing with a very serious personal situation at home and apologized for being less available than she should have been. The team took the rest of the meeting to talk through where the project was failing and how they could work together to be more proactive as a team moving forward.

Alyssa showed a lot of courage by initiating a hard and potentially uncomfortable conversation, and her colleagues showed their own courage in being willing to take responsibility for their lack of engagement in their shared project. Her colleagues saw that they had caused Alyssa distress and knew they needed to make it right, and it took them being open and willing, rather than guarded and defensive, to enable this to happen. In response, Alyssa's anger and resentment immediately softened and deflated. The team knew that they could trust Alyssa to be honest with them when similar situations arose in the future, and Alyssa gained increased trust in and respect for these two colleagues.

There's no need for judgment or condemnation in the process of taking responsibility and making repair. Alyssa didn't have to rake her colleagues over the coals, just like they didn't need to beat themselves up or go down a spiral of shame. The interaction between Alyssa and her colleagues would not have improved if they'd been hard on themselves or each other. Judgment would have only escalated their suffering. This is why we can't stress enough that when you practice taking responsibility, you must lean heavily on *compassion*. When you remember that we're all human and we all make mistakes, you're more likely to be open and more willing to take responsibility and make repairs. This feels better for everyone.

Watch for defensiveness, the blame game, and excuses. All three of these can happen quickly if you're not mindful. Instead, let mistakes be an opportunity for learning and growth. Ask yourself, *What is there for me to learn here?* Grow your empathy by imagining how you'd feel if you were in the other person's position. Don't forget to intentionally and compassionately tend to the shame and discomfort that naturally arise in such situations. Not just yours, but the people around you as well.

It is empowering to take responsibility. Owning our pieces is not about placing blame or getting people to see that we're right. It's about taking ownership for our feelings, our responsibilities, and where we have fallen short. The more we avoid taking ownership of our own lives, decisions, thoughts, actions, strengths, and weaknesses, the further we move away from our core values and beliefs. In essence, we abandon ourselves. When we take responsibility for our pieces and own up to the parts of the issue that belong to us, we're able to learn from our mistakes and shift our behavior going forward.

Navigating Feedback

Now that you're becoming more connected to yourself and others, you need to know how to gracefully accept or reject feedback. We get verbal and nonverbal feedback from others and the environment all the time:

- A friend makes an offhand comment that you always cancel plans.
- Your preteen says you're mean and unfair for not letting them have social media.
- Your partner complains that you're always on your phone and don't listen to them.
- Your sister comments, "Is that what you're wearing?" as you get in her car.
- A client wants you to be available to meet on Saturday.
- Your friends say you're going home too early when you want to skip the afterparty.
- You receive an eye roll from your waiter when you order a slice of chocolate cake.

Regardless of the form it takes, feedback can be prickly, stirring up all kinds of uncomfortable feelings. Often, we have some sort of reaction. We might immediately agree with the feedback, taking it on like it's the gospel truth, or we might become defensive and irate that someone would suggest such a thing.

We love the idea of "trying on feedback," almost as if it's a new dress we're trying on in the fitting room. People have their own truths, perspectives, and core values, which might differ from ours. Just because someone else shared their truth doesn't mean it's a fit for us. So, we try it on. We create space to evaluate the feedback with openness, curiosity, and nonjudgment in our self-reflection. The feedback might be a fit. Or maybe not.

For instance, when you "try on" the feedback that you "always cancel plans," you might find yourself thinking, *Eek, keeping commitments is not my strong suit, and I actually have been pretty flakey recently. Moving forward, I'd like to be more intentional about keeping my commitments to my friends.* In this case, the feedback fits. By acknowledging it without judgment, you're freed up to make repairs, if needed, and you can do something different moving forward.

Alternatively, sometimes the feedback doesn't fit. There's a real possibility that you hear feedback from someone and think, *While I see where they are coming from, their feedback is not an accurate assessment of me, my values, and my intentions.* In other words, you can decide which pieces of the feedback you want to keep, which you want to alter, and which you want to send out of the dressing room with the reject pile.

No need to get worked up or caught in shame, blame, or judgment. You connect with your truth, you address what needs to be addressed, and you move on.

Practice Validation

Validation is an important part of creating strong relationships with the people in your life. In a nutshell, validation communicates, "I see you. I hear you." It's understanding at least a small part of another person's reality in a nonjudgmental way. It's accepting that *you* have your own perceptions, beliefs, and feelings that make sense to you given your history and current life circumstances, and others have *their* own perceptions, beliefs, and feelings that make sense to them given their history and current life circumstances. It is the acknowledgment and acceptance of each person's individual identity.[49] When you receive validation from others, it helps you feel as though your emotions are normal and expected, which creates an instant sense of relief and belonging. Just like putting cooling aloe vera on a sunburn, validation acts as a soothing balm in times of distress.

Validation as a concept might sound simple enough, but it's not always easy to do, especially when there's stress or conflict. So, let's get clear on what validation is and is not.

First, validation is *not* the same as problem-solving. In couples therapy, we often see situations where one spouse feels as though they do the lion's share of the household chores. When they talk about the pain of carrying the load alone, their partner often responds by offering solutions: "I'd be happy to take the trash out every night if you would just ask" or "If you would just do the laundry and dishes every morning, things wouldn't pile up so much." As clinicians, we try to teach our clients to offer validation *before* jumping into problem-solving. So, instead of immediately trying to fix the issue, we may coach the listening partner to validate their spouse's experience: "I understand that you feel unsupported when I don't do my part at home" or "I hear you. You are doing so much to keep our lives going."

Validation is also *not* agreement. You can validate someone even if you don't agree with them. For example, imagine your teenage daughter expresses anger at you for not agreeing to a 1:00 a.m. curfew. You don't have to give in to the request or agree that all teens should be allowed to stay out until 1:00 a.m. to acknowledge her desire to be with friends, her wish for more independence, or her feelings of anger and disappointment. You can still hold your boundary and validate another person's feelings, wishes, or desires.

We all need to feel seen for who we are. When done well, validation feels reassuring, comforting, and encouraging, both when we receive it and when we give it. It's a necessary ingredient in helping us regulate our emotions. In contrast, when we're invalidated, we might question our experience or become dysregulated. Think about how you feel when someone says, "You have no reason to be so upset," "What is wrong with you?" or "It's not a big deal." Invalidation feels terrible.

So, how can we practice more validation in our relationships? Validation is a two-way street. When we validate, we want to ensure we're being as open and curious as possible, noticing any judgments that crop up in our minds and suspending those judgments if possible. We want to actively listen to what the other person is saying, rather than just remaining quiet, ready to pounce when it's our turn to speak. Good eye contact is important, but it's not a staring or glaring contest. And for goodness' sake, if someone is taking the time to be vulnerable and honest with us, we need to put our phones down. We want to pay attention to any feelings the other person is communicating, both verbally and nonverbally, and check in to see if we understand. This is done with simple sentences starting with "What I hear you saying is . . ." or "It sounds like you are feeling . . ."

We can communicate validation or invalidation with our words and body language. Here are some examples of what you may have observed or experienced in your relationships. Notice what comes up for you as you read them.

	Validation	Invalidation
Verbal	• "I get it." • "I hear you." • "I think I understand, but could you tell me more about ____?" • "Anyone would've felt that way." • "That's so hard. No wonder you're so upset." • "That sounds really scary."	• "You'll get over it." • "It's really not that bad." • "You think that's awful? Well, let me tell you about ____." • "You should feel grateful that . . ." • "At least it wasn't worse."

	Validation	Invalidation
Nonverbal	• Leaning into what the person is saying • Making eye contact • Softening your facial expression • Being present, without distraction • Nodding in understanding	• Turning away from the person • Being distracted by your phone or electronic device • Rolling your eyes • Having a blank or hardened facial expression

We wish we could tell you that every time you practice validation with others, you'll feel the benefits of being heard and understood. But that is not always going to happen. Just like you can't get it right 100 percent of the time, other people in your life aren't going to either, which means you will sometimes end up feeling invalidated. Invalidation is a painful experience. Unfortunately, if you ruminate about not being validated, exaggerate your complaints to receive validation, distance yourself and punish others until they validate you the way you want them to, or pout about it, this will lead to further invalidation. These behaviors not only cause you to abandon yourself, but they also damage your relationships.

In the absence of external validation, you can self-validate. If you're not sure how to do this, go back to those tuning-in practices we've talked about throughout this book. Imagine what you might say to a good friend, or consult the table above and apply verbal and nonverbal validation to yourself. All of this can be done with a healthy dose of self-compassion. After you self-validate, you might need to practice some of the other skills we've talked about in this chapter, particularly speaking truth and being vulnerable.

Learn to Navigate Conflict

It's time to get to one of our least favorite things about relationships: conflict. When we speak truth, take risks by being vulnerable, or ask for what we want and need, conflict is practically inevitable. However, many of us are conflict avoidant and will do almost anything to keep the peace.

We'll bet you have some sort of bodily reaction to the word *conflict*. Sit with that word for a moment. Do you notice anything internally? Is there a tightness in your jaw or chest? Do you feel as if your stomach is dropping down into your shoes? Do you want to hide, or is your body preparing for a fight? And what about when you're involved in conflict? What does it feel like in your body? For most of us, we can sum it up in one word: *discomfort*.

Conflict in general is not fun. We're not going to pretend it is. When we're in conflict, we generally experience "hot" emotions at first, leading to reactivity, irrationality, and a quick response, either fight, flight, or freeze. It's not surprising that many of us avoid conflict at all costs! At the same time, some of us might be comfortable with certain aspects of conflict, and a few of us might even enjoy arguing, no matter the outcome. We're all wired differently. And even that can cause conflict!

However, conflict is a natural part of any relationship, so learning to navigate conflict while also staying connected to ourselves is essential. We may be aware that something is "off" in our relationships, but it might be hard to identify what, specifically, that is. Or maybe we know exactly what is bothering us, but we don't know *how* to engage in what might be a difficult discussion. Many of us have not had good role models when it comes to effectively handling conflict, and we may struggle to express ourselves clearly when emotions are high.

In addition, there seem to be different playbooks for men and women. Men are conditioned not to show sadness, while women are conditioned not to show anger. Since conflict generally involves multiple emotions, including sadness and anger, *all* genders are at a disadvantage in being able to navigate conflict effectively if they're only allowed to express a small portion of emotions. Emotions are an important part of conflict but need to be managed well. That's where all the work you've done up to this point will come into play.

It requires a lot of skill to effectively manage conflict. You will need to be vulnerable and make space for others' vulnerability, have the self-awareness to make repairs when necessary, and take time to respond rather than react during more heated interactions. Being able to hold onto yourself while feeling emotionally activated takes patience and practice, while simultaneously navigating conflicting wants and needs with another person takes skill and effort.

As you work toward applying these communication skills in your daily life and relationships, keep in mind that, again, it isn't a matter of "mastering" a skill or getting everyone to see the situation as you do. Sometimes, when you speak truth and become more open and honest with the people around you, especially the people you love, it won't go smoothly. Connection and belonging are an ongoing practice, and relationships are complicated. Show yourself the same compassion you would want others to show you.

Do Try This at Home

#1: Connect with Your IGS

Ask yourself as often as possible:

- Who's in there?
- What does she want or need?
- How can I be a best friend to myself today?
- How can I be a first responder to myself?

#2: Practice Speaking Truth

Identify one place in your life where you could speak truth and try it out! Use the suggestions from the *Speaking Truth* section earlier in this chapter to guide you. Also notice when you're not speaking truth. This is a great opportunity to be curious about what's going on and what you might do differently.

#3: Look for Opportunities to Be Vulnerable, Take Responsibility, Make Repairs, or Validate

Is there one of these you're most interested in growing in your life? Or one of them you really need to work on? If so, dial in on that one!

Chapter 6

Navigating Self-Abandonment in Relationships

Between speaking truth, being vulnerable, taking responsibility and making repair, validating, and navigating conflict, it takes a lot of work to build strong bonds with other people! And on top of all that, it's easy to lose ourselves amid the inevitable ebb and flow of relationships. Remember, self-abandonment is something that typically happens gradually, over time, so the trick is to stay connected to ourselves, no matter what type of connection we're building with another person.

When we think of the ways we abandon ourselves in relationships, we think of the following: people-pleasing, caretaking, looking to experts and authority figures, blaming and being the victim, and being fiercely independent. We'll go through each of these examples in depth in this chapter, but keep in mind that underneath each is a problem with boundaries. Either we don't have strong enough boundaries or our boundaries are too rigid, thereby isolating us and keeping us disconnected. So, after we discuss these common types of self-abandonment, we will teach you how to optimize your boundaries to facilitate connection with others while remaining connected to yourself.

Five Types of Relationship Self-Abandonment

People-Pleasing

People-pleasing is essentially the act of suppressing your needs, wants, or interests to make others happy. You might hide or change parts of who you are to please others or avoid conflict, tension, or discomfort. This can happen in small ways, like agreeing to get Italian food when you really want sushi, but people-pleasing is often a slippery slope. In our private practices, we have seen women hide their political views from their loved ones for fear of making them angry, agree to take on huge responsibilities they do not have time for in an effort to be well-liked by their communities, or even stay in loveless marriages because they can't imagine letting their friends and family down by getting a divorce. People-pleasing means making choices that don't align with your values to preserve the peace or make someone else happy.

Underneath people-pleasing, there's often a fear of not being accepted by others, being disapproved of, or being judged. We already know that, as women, we're conditioned not to be threatening and not to be a burden. We may also have received messages that voicing our own needs makes us sound demanding or "bitchy."

You might be a people pleaser if:

- **You have difficulty saying no.** You say yes automatically, even when saying yes is a burden.
- **You feel resentful in your relationships.** Your resentment may stem from saying things you don't mean, such as "I don't mind staying home with the kids this weekend while you go hunting . . . again." This could also mean pretending to be someone you're not, like leaving your career to be a stay-at-home mom not because you want to, but because you think that would make everyone else happy.

- **You've gotten the feedback to "stop apologizing!"** Being afraid of conflict or disappointing others often goes along with people-pleasing, as does keeping quiet, withholding, and being avoidant.
- **You feel responsible for holding all the feelings in the room.** You jump in to try to make everyone feel better rather than allowing others to experience their own feelings and soothe themselves.
- **You experience significant discomfort when someone is upset.** You place the happiness of others over yourself to the point that you cannot enjoy yourself if someone you know and love is upset.

It's easy to fall into people-pleasing habits, so go easy on yourself. It's natural to want to avoid conflict and normal to want to be liked. No one wants to feel guilty for causing turmoil, and everyone needs validation from others. The other people in your life may have modeled people-pleasing behaviors for generations. We get it. It feels safer to go with the flow, not cause a fuss, and not take up too much space.

And people-pleasing does have its benefits. In the same way we get rewarded with praise when we manage all the things and work nonstop, we get rewarded when we please others. People pleasers can successfully avoid conflict and create a "pleasant persona." People pleasers are described as well-liked, dependable, and "nice." They may receive compliments for their hard work and selflessness. All of this feels good, and the rewards extend to the professional arena as well. Whether it's "doing our time" at an entry-level position, being a go-getter and getting recognized for a promotion, or building a solid reputation over the course of a long career, pleasing others has long-term benefits in the workforce. When used in this way, people-pleasing can be an effective strategy to build relationships and get our needs met.

People-pleasing works for us . . . until it doesn't. At some point, we've all been faced with decisions that require us to disappoint someone. For example, your boss taps you to lead an incredible new project, but it will mean you need to reschedule the family vacation. Your mom wants you to come to her house for Christmas, but your partner wants to spend the holiday break at home. In these examples, it's impossible to please everyone because it's physically impossible to be in two places at the same time. These situations are bound to happen. The trick is to learn to tolerate letting others down as you refuse to abandon yourself.

People-pleasing places your focus on how others might perceive you and on avoiding conflict. When you're distracted by thoughts like *What is everyone else thinking of me?*, it means you're tapped into your EGS. You're making decisions based on your desire to fit in, be liked, or avoid discomfort. All this outward focus blocks access to your IGS. Eventually, it becomes impossible to stand up for, or even be aware of, what you need.

When you focus entirely on the expectations of others, you inevitably become exhausted, depleted, and resentful. When you focus on how others perceive you, rather than tuning in to yourself and meeting your own needs or working toward your own desires and goals, you move further away from your true self. People-pleasing keeps you small, as do all the other forms of self-abandonment. Worse, it keeps you from creating real, solid connections with the people you care about.

Caretaking

We don't know you personally, but we're willing to bet you've done a *lot* of caretaking today. You might have made breakfast, packed lunches and planned dinner, ensured people were out of bed on time, run errands for your family, listened to a friend who was struggling, taken care of the animals, and shuttled children to and from various activities, just to name a few.

The three of us have done all those things today, and it's not even noon!

As we've alluded to, the role of caretaker is often the default role for women, and it's not something we necessarily choose. Rather, we've been conditioned to prioritize the wants and needs of others as more important than our own. We become caretakers for the people around us: our kids, partners, friends, coworkers, teachers, coaches, and even people we hardly know. In addition to relational caretaking, we can also caretake with tasks and logistics, as managers extraordinaire. From arranging summer childcare to planning a trip to visit the in-laws, we often end up taking care of everyone and everything—but ourselves.

Let's distinguish between care*giving* and care*taking*.[50] Caregiving involves offering care and support to someone in need and is driven by empathy and compassion. Conversely, caretaking is more about gaining approval or feeling needed, and it tends to get entangled with codependency. "Rescuing" and "fixing" are often part of caretaking. To be clear, we very much agree that offering care and support to someone in need is an important part of being a good human and is essential for having good relationships. When we *give* care, we do so from a place of being connected to ourselves and others. When we get caught in care*taking*, we often abandon ourselves in the process: It's impossible to stay connected to ourselves and our own wants and needs if we continually and automatically prioritize everyone else's wants and needs above our own.

When we're caught up in caretaking, we often feel like we know best or that we're the only one who can do ____ [*fill in the blank with anything—it's an amazingly exhausting choose-your-own-adventure*]. Taking care of everything for everyone, or even "just" some things for some people, creates a cycle when the more we do (or, really, overdo), the less others do. Talk about a perfect recipe for burnout and resentment! Many caretakers have a hard time asking for help. It's hard to accept help when we doubt others' ability to follow through.

We understand that taking care of others feels good. The problem is that although there are some payoffs to caretaking, when we over identify with this role, caretaking gets wrapped up with our worth: *I am a good person because I take care of everyone and everything.* It might even come to define our value in relationships: *I matter because of everything I do for others.* If our worth is largely contingent on us doing for others, there's not much space for us to do for ourselves.

Helpful Care*giving*	Unhelpful Care*taking*
• It gives me so much joy knowing that I'm able to take care of my family in the way that I do. I feel appreciated and valued. • I know that if I need to step back or ask for help that the people around me will be happy to provide it. • I expect others to be responsible for themselves and their actions. • I know there are moments when I need to prioritize my wants and needs, and I feel comfortable doing this.	• I'm expected to get everything done, and I get more resentful toward my partner, children, and friends every day. • My family has no idea how much I do for them, and let's be honest, they couldn't survive without my help. • If I wasn't taking care of others, I have no idea what I'd be doing. • I expect others to live up to my expectations. • I feel so guilty if I put my wants and needs ahead of others'.

There's another reason why you need to take it seriously when you overmanage other people and their feelings. Too much "just let me handle it" can undermine the people around you, as it sends an enabling and disempowering message that they are incompetent. Imagine how much you would want to help your partner if they were constantly telling you their way was the best way. We see this play out in relationships in one of two ways. First, this might lead the other person to under-function, which means you end up over-functioning to compensate. Alternatively, the other person might become resentful of you for being so controlling, thereby creating conflict and tension in the relationship. Not exactly the makings of a happy home, wouldn't you agree?

The bottom line is that caretaking takes too much from us. We eventually lose touch with ourselves. We miss out on opportunities to pursue our own dreams. We ignore opportunities to name and respond to our own needs and desires. Coming back to ourselves requires that we make space in our busy lives for ourselves, our wants, and our needs.

Looking to Experts and Authority Figures

One aspect of our EGS is the "expert" information we are inundated with on a daily basis. Whether it's looking to influencers for the best skincare regime, following our doctor's advice to lose weight, or reading every parenting book we can get our hands on, there's no shortage of advice about how to live our lives the "best" way.

There's absolutely nothing wrong with asking others for advice, consulting loved ones for their point of view, looking to experts or authority figures for information, or simply utilizing that super accessible online know-it-all, Google. The problem arises when engaging in those behaviors becomes a substitute for our IGS.

One reason we may overvalue experts and authority figures over our IGS is due to how self-assured, confident, and clear they seem. Who wouldn't want to trade uncertainty and discomfort for the assurance and certainty that an expert provides? Unfortunately, we often mistakenly equate confidence and certainty with competence.

Want to hear something crazy? According to organizational psychologist Tomas Chamorro-Premuzic, "The truth of the matter is that pretty much anywhere in the world men tend to *think* that they are much smarter than women. Yet arrogance and overconfidence are inversely related to leadership talent."[51] In other words, confidence and certainty actually have no bearing on whether someone actually knows what they're talking about. We're taking advice from people just because we misinterpret their confidence for intelligence. Imagine the ramifications of this in our personal lives and communities!

Here's something even scarier. In a 2010 TED Talk, economist Noreena Hertz explained the findings of an experimental MRI study where adults had their brains scanned as they listened to experts speak.

"As they listened to the experts' voices, the independent decision-making parts of their brains switched off. It literally flat-lined. They took whatever advice the experts said, however right or wrong."[52] Yes, you read that correctly. She said the parts of the brain responsible for independent decision-making *literally turned off* as soon as the expert's voice turned on.

You can probably guess why this happens: We want to avoid discomfort! It's easier, at least in the short term, to rely on others for guidance. However, we sometimes forget that experts can be wrong. Experts can also be wrong *for us* specifically. Although there might be truth to what they advise, it doesn't mean their guidance applies to our lives or is the best fit for us.

You make so many decisions every day. So do we! Decision fatigue is real, and relying on someone else to lighten your cognitive load can be important. However, when you spend your time endlessly seeking out opinions and researching before you take action, you can become overwhelmed. The work of staying grounded in who you are involves discerning when to go with your gut and when to rely on others to inform your decisions. You will get better at this as you do the important work of leveraging your IGS.

Blaming and Being the Victim

As you know from the previous chapter, admitting fault can result in a wave of self-judgment that is difficult to tolerate. As humans, we want to avoid these negative feelings, so we point the finger at someone or something else.[53] However, when we externalize blame or refuse to own up to our part in conflict, communication issues, or negative outcomes, we set ourselves up for continued self-abandonment in relationships. When we take on the victim role, when we get stuck in self-pity or carry the belief that everything happens *to* us, we relinquish control over our own lives and give our power away.

In relationships, whether personal or professional, we are not going to be perfect. Sometimes, when we stop and tune in, we may realize that we need to change our own behaviors. That realization can be painful, so we often try our best to avoid it. We've seen clients go to great lengths to blame their significant other for their marital issues, only to later recognize that they, too, hold some responsibility for the problems in the relationship. Ultimately, they have a choice: either own up to their part and make an effort to change the situation or remain stuck.

When we show up in close relationships feeling like we *can't* do anything to change our situation, we not only limit our opportunities for learning and growth, but we also likely frustrate our partners, family, and friends. By taking on the victim role, we often become avoidant, chronically passive, or help-rejecting complainers. We give our power away, and the imbalance of power puts a strain on our relationships. People quickly tire of others who are not trying to function on the same level as independent adults. People don't enjoy being blamed or dealing with a victim mentality and may ultimately choose to leave the relationship.

Those of us with a history of trauma or depression may have developed a sense of learned helplessness—the belief that we can't escape a negative situation and that it's impossible to help ourselves.[54, 55] You are not at fault for any of the terrible things that have happened in your history, and you may need support in the form of therapy to take ownership over your story, exercise more control over your life, and find a way forward. It's incredibly difficult to move past trauma, which reshapes how you see the world. Its impact can be lifelong. Trauma-informed treatment can provide you with a sense of safety and help you cope with these negative experiences. Even without a significant history of trauma, many people require extra help to move forward from the past.

At the end of the day, blaming others for your shortcomings can burn bridges. When you blame others, you put them on the defensive and rob yourself of the opportunity to problem-solve or directly address the issue at hand. Most importantly, you lose sight of the key components of relationships: empathy, vulnerability, and authentic connection to others. All of this makes for a very unsatisfying adult relationship.

Being Fiercely Independent

People-pleasing, caretaking, and looking to experts all orient us *outside* ourselves. They all involve overrelying on other people while we ignore ourselves. But guess what? These aren't the only ways that our conditioning causes us to lose sight of who we are. Fierce independence is on the other end of the spectrum. It's possible to become overly reliant on ourselves, refusing to allow anyone to see our vulnerabilities and, in turn, disconnecting from the people around us.

The concept of fierce independence has recently been described in the popular media as "hyper-independence" or "toxic hyper-independence."[56] The motto of a fiercely independent woman is "I can do it all myself," reminiscent of a toddler pushing for more autonomy with their declarations of "Me do it!"

Here are some factors that keep women trapped in a solitary prison of fierce independence:

Unhelpful beliefs about asking for support	"It's not okay to ask for help." "I'm weak and lazy if I need help."
Prior life experiences of being neglected or let down by others	"Others are unavailable." "I can't trust others to be there when I need them to be." "I need to take care of things on my own."
Fear of vulnerability and connection	"If I open up to or rely on others, I might end up hurt or disappointed. Or someone could use it against me."
Illusion of total control	"I don't have to depend on anyone. I can do it all myself."

It feels protective and safe to not have to depend on others, to not show "weakness" or humanity, and to avoid potential disappointment. But it's exhausting to have to do everything for ourselves, by ourselves. It ultimately feels like too much responsibility, which is heavy and overwhelming. In addition, we miss out on connection, support, and love. As much as we might fear being disappointed or let down, avoiding connection and opportunities for support causes us to miss out on people who can meet our needs, exceed our expectations, and lighten our load. Connection, closeness, and intimacy are formed by giving and receiving support. When we are fiercely independent, we bypass this natural give-and-take. We self-isolate, ending up lonely and anxious.

As with every other type of self-abandonment, fierce independence happens on a continuum. Self-sufficiency is great, but too much turns us into islands. When we're hyper-independent, we're cut off from connection with others, which limits our connection to ourselves. Humans are, by nature, social beings. We are wired for connection and community. Fierce independence requires us to silence our natural desires for closeness, intimacy, and love. In essence, we disconnect from our own humanity and ourselves.

Boundaries

A boundary is a line between "me" and "not me." We like to think of boundaries as being on a continuum. On one end, boundaries can be too loose, which results in us turning over our power to others and minimizing our wants and needs. When we have too few boundaries, we take responsibility for holding all the feelings in the room—everyone and everything is our responsibility, and it's hard to find "me." On the other end of the spectrum, rigid boundaries separate us from others and don't allow anyone to get close to us. When we have too many boundaries, we're like desert islands cut off from the rest of the world.

Boundary issues can both cause self-abandonment and be the consequence of abandoning ourselves. Therefore, working on our boundaries is a solution for self-abandonment in relationships. Some of us need to work on creating and enforcing boundaries, which allows us to better prioritize our own wants and needs. Others may need to work on loosening boundaries and opening up so we can form better connections. Many of us need to do a combination of these, depending on the situation and moment.

So, where do we begin? We bet you can guess where we're headed! You'll start the same place you always begin: by tuning in to your IGS. Your IGS helps you know if you need to set a boundary, what boundary you need to set, and with whom. As you're connecting with your IGS about boundaries, here are some helpful prompts to guide you:

- When you consider the situation in question, what's happening in your body?
- What feelings do you notice?
- Imagine how you might feel later if you set a boundary now. What if you *don't* set a boundary now?
- Do you notice any judgments getting in the way?
- What do you want?
- What do you need?

As a heads up, there might be a conflict among your wants and needs. *I feel overwhelmed* and *I want to make that sale. I feel stressed* and *I want to get a promotion while also spending more time with my family.* That's okay. Remember, it all belongs. You can make space for the contradictions as you listen for clarity around what sort of boundary you need to set to take care of yourself.

In working with women, we've found two main categories of boundaries to be essential in staying connected to ourselves while in relationship with others. In the next sections, we'll discuss those two essential boundaries and explore how you can integrate them into your own life and relationships.

Essential Boundary #1: Learn to Say No

Most of us can relate to our plates being "too full." Many of us are overly busy and overcommitted. In addition, we spend a lot of time and energy on things that we feel like we "have" to do, leaving us too depleted to invest in the things that really light us up. Burnout comes from saying yes too much, not saying no enough, and not saying yes to the *right* things. So, how do we empty our plates? How do we say no to the nonessential so that we have capacity to say yes to what matters most?

By learning the vital skill of saying no.

Saying no frees time, space, and energy for rest, fun, and connection. When we give ourselves permission to say no, we are far less likely to become resentful and burned out. Saying no when needed is a way to respect our IGS, allowing us to honor who we are, what we want, and what we need.

There are different types of situations where you can practice saying no. Sometimes, you can say no in response to an external trigger, such as when a request is made of you. For example, "Will you head the alumni committee?" or "Can you join us for a girls' weekend away?" Other times, you can say no in response to an internal trigger. For instance, you might realize you're uncomfortable with your in-laws letting your kid watch *Law and Order: SVU*, so you initiate a conversation about appropriate TV shows for an eleven-year-old. Or you realize you're tapped out, so you let your partner know you won't be making a homemade dinner tonight.

Often, saying no involves other people. But, sometimes, you have to say no to yourself: *I cannot add another thing to my to-do list. No more scrolling or googling. No, I cannot buy another pair of jeans. I've made the decision to stay at my job until the end of the year, so no more daily debate on whether I should leave now.* It can be hard to say no to yourself if you're bored, uncomfortable, or desperate to add some fun to your daily grind. *Sign me up for that eight-week self-help class even though my evenings are already packed. Baking cookies for tomorrow's meeting sounds much more fun than doing my taxes tonight.* You may say yes to an activity that is immediately gratifying, ultimately adding more to your plate and not really dealing with the issue at hand. Remember, staying overly busy is an avoidance technique that ultimately leads to self-abandonment.

It can be easy to forget that "no" is even an option. Saying yes can feel like an automatic response when you don't take the time to tune in and determine how you want to proceed. At other times, you may feel uncertain about how to clearly turn down a request. Lastly, there are instances when you don't have the opportunity to actually say no because you're never asked in the first place—your "yes" is just assumed.

You may feel like something bad will happen if you say no—that the task won't be completed correctly or that you might disappoint people who are counting on you. You may also encounter resistance to your "no." The person on the receiving end may refuse to accept your boundary or get angry and upset if you don't go along with the plan. Or you may not realize you're a "no" until after you've said yes, and it feels too late to change your answer.

These are tough situations, all of which require you to tune inward. Take a moment to think about your life. Where do you say yes when you really mean no? Where in your life do you need to set a boundary by saying no? And to whom?

Here are some examples of boundaries in service of saying no. See if any of them resonate.

- **Work**
    - I don't respond to emails after 7 p.m. or on the weekends.
    - I'm not able to complete that presentation this week.
    - I won't be able to travel to a meeting out of town that day.

- **Extracurriculars and friends**
    - I'm not interested in serving on that committee this year.
    - I can't attend your wedding shower.
    - I'm not able to spend $2,000 for the girls' weekend.
- **Family**
    - We won't be hosting Thanksgiving for the whole family this year.
    - [*To your child*] I won't be making your lunch this school year.
    - I will not be paying your electric bill.
- **Physical safety and basic needs**
    - I don't want to be touched like that.
    - Take your hands off me.
    - I can't stay out late tonight; I'm going to bed early.
- **Emotional safety**
    - I'd appreciate it if we could change the topic from dieting.
    - If you continue to speak to me this way, I will have to leave.
    - I cannot discuss my dating life any further with you.

Many women struggle with saying no, and they end up overcommitted, exhausted, and depleted. However, there are other instances when we need to say yes rather than saying no. Most often, we see this with the seemingly "optional" things in life: social connection, adventures, pleasurable activities, and leisure pursuits. Perhaps we've come to overvalue productivity and work, so we decline opportunities for fun, play, and connection. Or we've spent so many years alone or with the kids that we've lost touch with friends, and it feels awkward to reach out. Or we're just so exhausted and burned out that we don't have the energy to do anything else, no matter how fun it might be. However, boundary setting also means saying yes to things that light us up!

It can be hard to strike the balance of saying yes in combination with saying no, to create time, space, and energy for thriving. A helpful place to start is to ask your IGS, "What have I been neglecting?" Once you have clarity around this, you can better determine what you *want* to say yes to and what you *need* to say no to in order to make this happen.

Essential Boundary #2: Ask for Help, for What You Want, and for What You Need

As we discussed in chapter five, community provides a needed sense of belonging. Another vital benefit of community is support. We simply *can't* do it all alone. We all need help, both pragmatically and emotionally, yet it can be so hard for us to ask for it. As a result, many women end up trying to do too much on their own. As you already know and are likely experiencing, this leads to burnout, exhaustion, overwhelm, resentment, and isolation. Asking for help can range from asking someone to watch your kids to reaching out for emotional support when you've had a bad day to pushing back a work deadline.

There are plenty of things going on inside of us that make it hard to ask for help. There's the self-judgment: *I'm weak and incompetent if I can't do it on my own. I don't deserve help. I'm not worthy.* There's the desire to fix, plan, and control: *They won't do it right, so I have to do it myself.* There's the victim mentality, where we expect others to read our minds: *If they really cared about me, they'd know I need help. I shouldn't have to ask.*

In addition to the negative thoughts we have about ourselves, we may also fear how others might respond to our requests for help. We fear we'll be a burden: *It'll be an inconvenience for them. What if they say yes but they really don't want to help? What if it creates too much work, stress, or strain for them?* We fear others will judge us as pushy, selfish, or needy: *I know they're thinking, "I can't believe she asked me for help. Who does she think she is?*" Lastly, we fear potential rejection: *What if they say no? That would be so humiliating.*

We create these stories while forgetting how *we* feel when others ask us for help or support. Most of us feel honored when someone confides in us or asks us to help, and we feel good about ourselves when we do nice things for other people. People typically *want* to help, and research shows that helping others boosts our mood, increases connection, and reduces stress.[57, 58] In other words, when we ask someone for help, we give them the opportunity to do something that will most often make *them* feel better. Why would we want to deprive them of this good feeling by not asking for help? Also, when we ask others for help, we implicitly give them permission to ask us for help later down the road. Everyone wins. We can all give and receive support.

Please remember this: We are always allowed to ask for help. When we ask for help, our lives feel easier. We have more time and energy for what matters most to us. We don't feel as burdened or alone. We feel closer and more connected to others in our lives, growing our community of support.

This is also an opportunity to set a boundary by asking for what we want or need. It's hard for us women to acknowledge and name our wants and needs, even to ourselves. It's even harder to speak those wants and needs aloud! Often, we'd prefer that people could read our minds so that we wouldn't have to ask. And since people are not mind readers, we end up disappointed and frustrated.

To illustrate, let's revisit Maria, our fifty-year-old single mom who happens to have found a wonderful boyfriend. She is upset that this wonderful boyfriend hasn't offered to pick her up from the airport next week, and she shares her frustration with a friend, who asks, "Have you directly asked him to pick you up?" Maria says she made it clear by commenting to him that she wasn't sure how she was going to get home from the airport. "How much clearer could I have been? Do I have to spell it out for him?" Her friend chuckles and says, "Yes, Maria. Yes, you do. You need to spell it out directly for him." After brainstorming how she might phrase this, Maria approaches her boyfriend that night and asks, "Hey, honey, any chance you could pick me up from the airport next Wednesday around 8 p.m.?" He says he'd be happy to.

As seen with Maria, it's vital that we be clear and direct rather than expecting others to guess, infer, or read between the lines. It's not fair or realistic to expect others to read our minds. And despite whatever conditioning you may have experienced, asking for what you want or need is not being impolite or too forward. It's taking responsibility for meeting your wants and needs, which serves both you and your relationships.

Self-Compassion: Let's Make It Fierce!

Setting boundaries can be scary and hard. And as with all discomfort you encounter in life, you will most definitely want to harness the tender, warm, nurturing, and soothing type of self-compassion we've talked about throughout this book. But you'll also want to tap into another type of self-compassion known as *fierce self-compassion*. Coined by self-compassion expert Kristin Neff, fierce self-compassion is akin to "momma bear" energy that enables you to take action to effectively care for and protect yourself and the people you love.[59]

Fierce self-compassion is the ability to motivate yourself to act when needed, even when it feels hard. It's a more energizing force and requires *doing* something, often something that's observable to people from the outside. Fierce self-compassion calls on immense courage and draws on kindness rather than judgment. You use fierce self-compassion in most of the communication and boundary skills we've talked about thus far: speaking truth, being vulnerable, taking responsibility, saying no and yes, asking for help, and asking for what you want and need. Many of these things are inherently challenging, so they require *fierce* self-compassion to push through feelings of discomfort and do what's needed to reduce your suffering.

For example, if you notice that you are feeling lonely and disconnected, you may need to access fierce self-compassion to motivate you to reach out to people and connect, even when it feels awkward and anxiety-provoking. Or, if your IGS reveals certain habits are not working for you, be it using substances, overworking, spending money, or staying up too late scrolling on social media, you'll need to stand up to yourself and hold yourself accountable for changing the problematic behavior.

You may also need to access fierce self-compassion when you stand up to other people. Perhaps your boundaries have been repeatedly disregarded, or certain people in your life continually treat you or your loved ones with disrespect. In such instances, you may need to access fierce self-compassion to end a friendship, go "no-contact" with a family member, or leave a marriage. When you connect with fierce self-compassion, you feel brave and empowered, which propels you to take action to protect and care for both yourself and those you love.

To identify where you need to create boundaries with fierce self-compassion, ask yourself these questions:

1. What boundary violation is occurring in which you feel anger, frustration, resentment, or fear?
2. Where do you need to take action to care for, protect, or motivate yourself or someone else?
3. What can you say to stand up for yourself? Imagine a friend in a similar situation. What would you say on their behalf?
4. Are you able to remind yourself that boundary setting is an act of self-care?

Prepare for Pushback

Not everyone around you will be happy about your new and improved boundaries. Some people in your life have gotten used to you showing up in a certain way, and they're likely to resist you trying something different, especially if it means that they're going to have to start doing things differently too. If the people in your life are used to you being agreeable, they're going to get their feathers ruffled when you start standing up for yourself. They may be used to you always offering to help and may react poorly if you start asking for support too. That is all okay.

When navigating those tough situations, remember there's a system around you that's built on you doing things the way you've always done them, and the system will adjust and recalibrate as you start to do things differently. Give yourself permission to experiment and discover what is most important to you in life. You know what you need and what you want. We hope you're learning that you're uniquely qualified to take care of yourself.

Executing boundaries can be incredibly difficult, and that's why we saved this topic for later in the book, after you've done so much internal reflection and so much work on staying connected to yourself. Many of us struggle with following through. We may hit barriers such as guilt, anxiety, or pushback that make us back down from setting the boundary.

The bottom line is that boundary setting is an ongoing process and takes practice. Depending on the nature and duration of the problem and the other people involved, you may need to set the same boundary multiple times. Talk about frustrating! It's natural to want to give up when the results don't match your expectations, but you cannot measure your success based on the response of others. Boundaries are successful when they allow you to hang on to your integrity, and it's important to have realistic expectations and not give up too soon.

Boundary-Setting Tips

Boundaries create space, allowing you to reconnect with the parts of yourself you've abandoned. They are critical to making room for yourself in your own life. We want to make sure you're successful when you're setting boundaries, so here are our top ten tips to help you be as effective as possible:

1. **Utilize the power of the pause.** Delaying doesn't mean waiting forever. It means "I need time to think about this." If your default is to say yes when someone asks you to do something, this is especially important for you. Very few situations require an immediate response, even though it might feel like it. So, before you make another commitment, slow down. Take time to look at your calendar and review your priorities before deciding. This means that you are going to take time to reflect and tune in to your IGS before you say anything! Taking a beat is not license to avoid, so be sure to circle back with your answer in a reasonable amount of time.
2. **Say "I have a policy . . ."** This makes saying no less personal because you're saying no on a general principle, not based on the specific request or person. For example, "I have a policy that kids don't swim in our pool without an adult present," "I have a policy that I don't work on my vacation days," or "I have a policy that I don't check email after 6 p.m. or on weekends." Make sure your policies reflect *your* priorities and values.
3. **Do it in writing.** Sometimes, texts and emails can be your best friends by allowing you the time and space to create an effective "no" by using precise and direct language. This also affords physical distance, which helps you resist pushback or efforts to talk you into forgoing your boundary.

4. **Rehearse and role-play.** Nervous about setting a particular boundary? It can be really helpful to do a practice run either with yourself in front of the mirror or with a trusted friend. Rehearsing also helps settle your nervous system, and being grounded and calm helps such conversations go better.
5. **Be consistent.** This one is especially important if you get pushback. You may need to repeat your boundaries several times before people realize you're serious. And this probably goes without saying, but once you've stated what you're going to do, make sure to follow through.
6. **Know that you're allowed to change your mind.** We know this sounds like the opposite of tip #5, but stay with us here! Even if you've initially said yes or no, you haven't made a binding contract with the devil. You have a right to change your mind. Sometimes, circumstances change, which results in you needing something different. When you stay connected to yourself, you can always pivot to align with your IGS.
7. **Start small.** Build up your courage for more difficult "nos" by starting small. Practice in situations that are low stakes. For example, tell your kid they can't wear a swimsuit to play in the snow, tell your friend you don't want to go to their proposed restaurant and suggest another, or tell your boss you can't go to a meeting because you have a dentist appointment during work hours. The purpose is to practice saying no effectively and confidently.
8. **Consider the many "nos" you've been given.** We bet you've had invitations turned down, requests rejected, or romantic disappointments occur. Was it really *so* terrible? Did you end up hating the person who told you no? The fact that you can handle someone else's "no" is proof that people can withstand your "no" and still be okay.

9. **Create a mantra.** By now, you know we love mantras! These are positive statements you repeat to yourself to motivate, encourage, or calm yourself. Here are some examples related to boundary setting:

   - *It's okay to say no.*
   - *I've got this.*
   - *It's my divine right to say no.*
   - *I can handle whatever happens.*

   What's a mantra that fits for you?

10. **Make your timing intentional.** Choose the right time. If you anticipate that a boundary conversation is going to be difficult, choose a moment when you (and the other person, if possible) are calm, rested, sober, and not distracted. Additionally, give people time to adjust. If setting boundaries is new for you, and you used to say yes to every request, others may be shocked when you start saying no or standing up for yourself. There might be some people in your life who resist your attempts to set boundaries, but most people will be supportive after you've given them time to adjust.

And always keep in mind that people might not like your boundaries. They might not respond as you wish they would. That's okay. Connect with your IGS and practice self-compassion to help you tolerate the discomfort.

Do Try This at Home

#1: Set a Boundary

Think of a very clear and specific boundary you could set in the next few days. Try it out and see how it goes. Consult the previously discussed *Boundary-Setting Tips* for added support. Remember to practice self-compassion along the way!

#2: Ask for Help

What do you need help with today? Who can you ask to support you? Inventory the people in your life: Who is reliable, dependable, and trustworthy? If you have difficulty asking for help, start higher up on that list.

#3: Ask for What You Want or Need

Identify something you want or need today. Who can help you fulfill that want or need? Make your request by clearly and directly asking the other person for what you want or need. You've got this!

Chapter 7

Upgrade Your Thinking

We have spent the majority of this book encouraging you to connect with your body and IGS. In other words, everything below your neck. We've focused on embodiment strategies because they play such an essential role in our ability to reconnect with ourselves after self-abandonment. These practices are new for many of us and require practice.

However, we can't ignore the other aspect of our experience that happens between our ears: our thoughts. In chapter three, we talked about how getting stuck in our heads disconnects us from our bodies and our intuition, but we would be remiss if we didn't dive a little deeper into how certain thinking traps can lead to self-abandonment.

What, Exactly, Are Thinking Traps?

Whether it's getting caught up in unrealistic expectations, comparing ourselves to others, holding perfectionistic standards, or telling ourselves stories that ultimately trip us up, "thinking traps," also known as cognitive distortions, fracture and filter our experiences. In the following section, we offer you additional insights into four main thinking traps so that you can sidestep these pitfalls and remain connected to yourself. Some of these will apply to you and some won't. That's okay. It's not as important to identify *which* thinking traps you fall into as it is to simply *notice* when your thoughts are disconnecting you from your IGS.

Unrealistic Expectations

Alyssa, whom we introduced in chapter three, had imagined the most wonderful adventure when she moved to New York City after college. She thought it would be fabulous: a prestigious job, exciting nightlife, fabulous new friends, romance, and so much newness to explore. Unfortunately, New York did not live up to her expectations. With so many hours spent at work, she had limited time and energy to explore the city—and even when she did have time to socialize, she didn't have much luck in making new friends. The few dates she'd had were total busts. Alyssa found herself very disappointed.

The gap between what we expect and what actually happens creates a lot of uncomfortable feelings, including disappointment, irritability, frustration, anger, and resentment. You probably don't have to think back too far to remember a time when your actual experience didn't measure up to your expectations.

Expectations are our beliefs about how things *should* unfold—what we imagine and what we *believe* we know to be true. We have expectations about ourselves: our performance, our goals, our hopes and dreams, our appearance, and our leisure time. We also have expectations about others: what our partner should be like, how our kids should act, how our friends and family should show up for us, and how we should be treated at work. You'll notice expectations sound like rules with an abundance of shoulds, oughts, and musts. Some of these scripts are rigid and rule-based, while others are driven by daydreams and hopes, tapping into our wants or desires.

In addition, our expectations often sound definitive. You rarely hear someone say, "Our upcoming beach vacation is probably going to be fine—there will be some good points but likely also some struggles" or "I think it's great my little Johnny is scraping by with a C." No, our expectations tend to use black-and-white language, and they are often tied to a specific outcome: "This beach vacation is going to be the most fabulous and romantic experience ever" or "My son better be working as hard as possible, getting those A's I know he's capable of."

The tricky part about expectations is that we're not always aware of them. Sure, at times our expectations are very clear and match reality. These are instances where we've consciously decided on and voiced an expectation, like our kids' curfews: "You need to be home by midnight tonight."

However, more often, expectations are unspoken and are lurking in our subconscious. *Mothers should always get up with the baby in the middle of the night. The house must be perfectly clean when company arrives.* When we can't put words to our expectations, we can't work with them, even though they continue to impact us both on an individual and relational level. For example, if you have the subconscious expectation that a mom "should" always get up with the baby in the middle of the night, you may experience a feeling of lonely frustration whenever your husband snoozes blissfully through a 3 a.m. feeding.

Tap into curiosity and your IGS to put words to your expectations. This enables you to work with them directly. Do you really believe the mom should be solely responsible for the baby's middle-of-the-night awakenings? Is it okay for a mom to want or need help? In addition to acknowledging your expectations to yourself, you need to speak them aloud to others. For instance, you may be aware that you expect family members to pitch in with chores around the house, but if you never communicate this expectation with them, you'll be continually frustrated when they don't help like you want. Once you name the expectation, you create space to be more curious and open about it. You can make an informed decision about whether or not this expectation is serving you at this particular moment and, if not, you can ditch or rework the unhelpful expectation.

In many instances, high expectations can motivate us to strive and grow, and they can propel us forward. On the flip side, low expectations can lead us to be pleasantly surprised when things turn out better than expected. Is it just us, or are the best nights the ones that happen spontaneously when you really weren't expecting much at all? However, if our expectations are too low, we may accept mistreatment or avoid setting important boundaries.

When we notice and name our expectations, we free ourselves up to respond more skillfully. In doing so, we might need to readjust our beliefs: *I'm not on board with the idea that the mom is in charge of all middle-of-the-night awakenings for the baby, so I'm going to talk with my husband about creating a plan that includes both of us sharing this responsibility*. We might need to level up our self-compassion, making space for all the feelings that arise when life falls short of our hopes and dreams. In Alyssa's case, this meant grieving the loss of her perfect New York City fantasy and recognizing where she was dissatisfied and needed to make changes.

Expectations are neither good nor bad, right nor wrong. The trick is to become more aware of our expectations and how they impact us.

Questions to Help You Escape the Expectation Trap

1. Do you have any unspoken expectations? Are you operating under any expectations that you don't agree with? Are there any expectations you can put words to?
2. Are your expectations realistic? Do they serve you? If not, can you simply drop the expectation or upgrade to something more realistic and helpful?
3. How do you respond when your expectations are not met? Do you fall into self-criticism, judgment, resentment, frustration, anger, or disappointment? If so, how can you cope? (Hint: Drop or readjust your expectation [see #2], practice being flexible, or practice self-compassion and letting it all belong.)

4. How tightly do you hold this expectation? How attached are you to a certain outcome? Can you practice acceptance and soften your expectations, focusing more on how things actually are versus how you want them to be?

Comparisons

From the moment we're born, we are placed on the "growth chart" of comparison. It starts with height, weight, and head circumference as infants and, as we develop, the comparisons seemingly grow to all aspects of our lives. Societal norms and expectations are huge drivers of comparisons. As you know by now, we all want to belong—it's our number one psychological need. We want to be part of the pack, so scanning the group to find out exactly where we stand helps us do just that.

To be sure, comparisons aren't all bad. Comparing ourselves to others can help us feel less alone. Comparisons can also motivate us to improve. However, overrelying on comparisons to measure our self-worth keeps us dialed into our EGS and disconnected from our IGS.

There are two different types of comparisons that can keep us disconnected: upward and downward comparisons. Upward comparisons occur when we compare ourselves to others whom we deem as "better than" us in some way, often intensifying our feelings of not-enoughness: *She's so put together. I feel like an absolute slob standing next to her. Geez, her house is so organized and clean. I'm lucky if I can put away the laundry a week after I take it out of the dryer. Why are her kids so polite and well-behaved? I feel like I should be given the Mother of Heathens award.*

Upward comparisons make us "shrink down" and feel bad about ourselves, but they can also breed envy and resentment in our relationships. Envy generally occurs when we compare ourselves to others who are similar to us in some way, perceiving them as some sort of threat. To protect our sense of self, we might engage in judgment and blame. We might also complain to others about how unfair things are, ruminate about what we don't have, withdraw and distance ourselves in our relationships, or even find satisfaction in seeing others fall from grace. Not necessarily the makings of authentic connection to self or others, right?

In contrast, downward comparisons are used when we compare ourselves to others we deem as worse off or less than ourselves. Oftentimes, we use these comparisons to remind ourselves to be grateful. For example: *I'm pissed that I didn't get a promotion, but my friend's company just laid her off, so I guess I should feel grateful that I still have a job at all.* However, when we compare our suffering in this way, we can feel like we don't "deserve" to experience any disappointment or pain because we should be grateful instead. In essence, we invalidate our own experience and don't feel better or grateful in the long term.

We can also use downward comparisons to make us feel better about our circumstances. For example: *I make way more money than my colleague does* or *My kids are so much smarter than hers.* When we "puff up" ourselves in this way, we may feel better in the moment, but those feelings are usually temporary. In extreme cases, these types of downward comparisons can lead to overconfidence and arrogance, which negatively impact our relationships.

Whether social comparisons cause us to "shrink down" or "puff up," they generally result in more self-doubt than ever before, keeping us in a constant state of self-abandonment. This can lead to a vicious cycle of looking outward and leaning on that pesky EGS to manage the unwanted feeling of self-doubt. As you know by now, looking outside ourselves only creates a more unsteady and shaky sense of self.

Questions to Help You Sidestep the Comparison Trap

1. In what areas of your life do you find that you're comparing yourself to others? Why is this so important to you?
2. What do you feel when you compare yourself to others? Does your self-doubt and not-enoughness increase or decrease?
3. How can you acknowledge your own worth today?
4. Rather than compare yourself to others, can you focus on doing something meaningful or enjoyable instead?

Perfectionism

Would you consider yourself a perfectionist? Does your competitive streak come out more than you would like? Are you afraid that if you don't hold yourself to the highest possible standard, something terrible will happen?

Perfectionism is the intense need and desire to do everything right and perfectly. That same not-enoughness that underlies all forms of self-abandonment can push us to attempt to perform every task perfectly, avoid failure at all costs, and display a perfect persona to the outside world. Perfectionism can be hard to shut down because, like so many other types of self-abandonment, it is constantly reinforced by external validation.

Many of us use perfectionism to manage our anxiety, circumvent discomfort, and exercise control. Perfectionism does a great job of distracting us from negative feelings when we convince ourselves, *If I do this perfectly, nothing bad will happen.* For example, if you get caught up in hosting the "perfect" wedding for your daughter, you can ignore your feelings of sadness about your daughter growing up, your worries about your changing relationship, or even your mixed feelings about her new in-laws. Instead, you attempt to control the situation by micromanaging every aspect of the wedding. By focusing on its perfect execution, you get caught in your head and don't have to process your feelings or live in the moment.

Spoiler alert: Perfection isn't actually attainable for us mere mortals. Striving for perfection and trying to reach the unreachable disconnects us from our feelings, and it also sets us up for a landslide of self-criticism. Imagine how you'd feel if and *when* something goes wrong at the "perfect" wedding you're trying to host. All those feelings you've been trying to avoid are likely to come rushing to the surface along with a side of harsh judgment.

Perfectionism also leads to black-and-white thinking, in which there is no gray area. In such a headspace, mistakes feel disastrous. If our performance isn't flawless, we believe we are a total failure. Striving for perfection inevitably keeps our focus outward, and dichotomous thinking fuels our belief that others will only approve of work that is perfectly executed. All of this keeps us trapped in an all-or-nothing thought process and focused on our EGS. Negative feedback feels intolerable, and any criticism causes us to spiral into shame, leaving no room for our humanity.

We're curious: How many "perfect" people do you enjoy spending time with?

This question has been a game changer for many of our clients. We love the people we love *because* they are human, not *in spite of* their humanity. In this book, we've talked a lot about the importance of authenticity in relationships, and you can imagine how perfectionism affects our ability to truly connect with one another.

There is nothing wrong with wanting to do well, achieve, and excel. However, when our aim is perfection, we become so focused on the end result and how we are perceived by the outside world that we can't enjoy or even fully *experience* the process of reaching our goals. We may think that striving for the highest possible standard is the only way to get ahead, but in the end, perfectionism may actually make our ultimate long-term goals more difficult to reach.

It is important to remember that failure often paves the way to success. Motivation is easier to maintain when you take note of compliments and celebrate your successes along the way. When you're tempted to hold on to impossibly high expectations and feeling terrified about what would happen if you were to let go, remember that you are *more* likely to reach your long-term goals when you allow yourself to be human and hold yourself with compassion.

Practices to Help You Ditch the Perfectionism Trap

1. Simply observe the perfectionistic thought. Perhaps you notice thoughts of not-enoughness, the pressure to be perfect, or a worry that bad things are going to happen.
2. What feelings are coming up in your body? Fear, anxiety, disappointment, frustration, sadness, shame? Put your hand on your heart and acknowledge your feelings, letting them all belong.
3. Practice compassion by stating, "I am human, so of course I'm not perfect. It's okay to make mistakes." Find whatever soothing phrase fits you.

Stories That Trip Us Up

Our minds are meaning-making machines, constantly trying to put the puzzle pieces together and make sense of what's happening around us. We're the most prolific writers ever—churning out abundant stories all day long, all in our minds. A driver cuts us off: *What an asshole.* A teenager doesn't unload the dishwasher: *She's lazy and selfish and doesn't care about our family.* A client cancels an appointment: *I'm such a horrible therapist, and my practice is going to fall apart.* Story after story after story. Endlessly.

It is important to notice our stories because they can greatly affect how we feel and how we show up in the world. Let's say Isabel's husband is away on a business trip and not texting as often as she would like. If Isabel tells herself the story, *He's having an affair with a coworker, or, at minimum, looking at porn all night*, she's likely to feel devastated and angry. If she tells herself the story, *I don't really matter to him. We're a lost cause. Couples counseling is never going to work, and I just know we're going to get a divorce*, she'll feel anxious and sad. Or if she tells herself the story, *He must be really busy on this work trip. I hope he's not too stressed and overwhelmed*, she'll likely feel more neutral, perhaps even with a side of empathy and compassion.

Sometimes, our stories can be helpful (*I can't drink caffeine after noon or I'll be up all night*), and sometimes they can limit our experiences (*I'm just not cut out to apply for that promotion*). Quite often, these limiting stories start with phrases like "I don't like . . ." or "I can't do that" or "I am . . ." Additionally, we can tell ourselves stories that make it hard to tune in to ourselves: *Having fun isn't as important as being productive* or *I'll never be accepted if I don't look a certain way* or *It's my job to make everyone happy*. These stories can understandably interfere with our IGS.

Stories often happen on an unconscious and automatic level. One of our jobs as psychologists is to help clients become more aware of the stories running amuck in their minds. We help them make the unconscious conscious. If we can practice catching and naming our stories, we're at a great advantage. We can then make informed choices about which stories serve us and which don't. About which we want to hold onto, which we want to revise, and which we want to send up in metaphorical flames.

Not only do our stories impact how we feel individually, but our stories greatly impact our relationships. Dr. Becky Kennedy, author of *Good Inside*, talks about "Least Generous Interpretations" (LGIs) versus "Most Generous Interpretations" (MGIs).[60] She's really talking about the stories we tell ourselves. For example, if we go to the dentist's office and wait forty-five minutes for our appointment, we might be tempted to create a story with the least generous interpretation: *This whole office is totally incompetent and poorly run. They totally suck and are being so inconsiderate.* This particular story will likely lead to anger and resentment, and we might end up being snippy and unkind with the office staff. LGIs lead to disconnection, both from ourselves and others.

Alternatively, we could craft a story drawing from an MGI: *Wow, it's really busy here today. I wonder if there were some unexpected stressors or issues with other patients or the dentist's family. I hope everyone's okay.* This story engenders a much calmer nervous system. We'll feel much more at peace and not as irritated or annoyed. And by the way, we can create a story that acknowledges and makes space for our very real feelings: *Gosh, I notice I'm feeling frustrated and annoyed that I have to wait for so long. It's hard when life doesn't go according to plan, and I'm feeling tempted to make up some nasty stories about everyone in this office. Perhaps I'll instead go check in with the front desk to get more information.*

Naming our stories and sharing them with others is a powerful strategy for leveling up our relationships. Often, we'll find that our stories are inaccurate, and talking about them can improve communication, trust, and connection with our loved ones. You can begin the conversation by starting with "I'm telling myself the story that . . ." For example, let's say you're concerned about a recent change in communication frequency with your sister and, without any evidence, have created a story that she's upset with you. Once you catch that story, you can approach her and say, "I'm telling myself the story that you're annoyed with me and don't want to talk to me." By checking in, you're clearing up a possible inaccuracy about your relationship, showing concern about your connection, and building closeness.

The good news here is that our stories are of our own creation. We make them up. We're the authors. So, when we stumble upon a story that doesn't work for us for whatever reason, we have the option to upgrade the story. The trick is staying connected and tuned in to how we're feeling, what we're thinking, who we are, and what we want and need, using the strategies we've covered so far in this book. This connection with ourselves helps us find the balance between our thinking brain and feeling heart.

Questions to Help You Level Up Your Stories

1. What story are you telling yourself at this moment?
2. Does this story feel helpful, harmful, or neutral?
3. What wants and needs are underlying this story? How might you directly give voice to those and get them met?
4. If this story isn't serving you or your relationships, what can you say to yourself that would be kinder and more effective?

Giving Yourself Permission

Now that you've become more aware of the thinking traps that disconnect you from your IGS, what can you do next? You can give yourself permission. Permission to do what, you ask? Permission to do and think differently.

We often don't do things differently because we don't feel like we're "allowed" to flip the script, color outside the lines, or live outside the box. But as grown adults, who else will give us permission if not ourselves? We've talked extensively already about the detrimental impact of looking outside of ourselves for validation and approval. Giving ourselves our own "permission slips" is another way of connecting to our IGS. Remember when you had to turn in permission slips at school? It's the same idea here, except now you can give yourself your *own* permission slip to do things or think differently.

Permission to Change Your Mind

Many of us believe that when we make a commitment to do something, we've entered into an unchangeable, binding contract. People are counting on us and expect us to follow through, so we believe we absolutely must do what we promised. While it's important to keep our word, when we feel like we're *never* allowed to change our minds or change directions, we can feel boxed in and tied down. And as you can imagine, this is a quick path away from ourselves and toward the expectations of others.

Staying connected to ourselves means taking the time and space to tune in to our IGS and acknowledge when we need to change our minds. Can you think of any examples from your own life? Maybe you said yes to a Friday night dinner back on Monday when you were feeling energized and rested from the weekend. By the time you get to Thursday night, however, it's clear that you're in need of some down time. Could you give yourself permission to change your mind? To change plans and do what feels right for you? You may worry that canceling dinner plans or breaking a commitment will lead you to let others down or disappoint important people in your life, but staying connected to yourself sometimes requires prioritizing your own wants or needs.

Do you give yourself space to check in to determine what's working for you? Maybe you set up a work schedule you thought was going to be great for you and your family, but by Wednesday night every week, you're feeling exhausted and dreading the next day. Or maybe you crafted a carpool routine that seemed efficient and easy back in August, but by the middle of October, you're worn out and feeling frazzled. Do you fall into the sunk-cost fallacy, where you feel like you need to stay committed once you've spent significant time, effort, or money into doing something a certain way?[61] Or could you give yourself permission to change your mind?

There may be some comfort in sticking with "the devil you know" and continuing with the way you've always done something. Again, this work is about finding a way to make decisions with your true, authentic self in the driver's seat. If your IGS is telling you it's time for a change, it's important to listen. As you know, ignoring your gut feeling and silencing your inner wisdom is the epitome of self-abandonment.

Permission to Experiment

Children are amazing to observe. They naturally embody a "beginner's mindset," showing up with openness and curiosity. They're eager to learn, eager to try new things, and not so bogged down with fears or judgments around making a mistake or not getting it "right." But something changes as we age. Our adult selves want to be experts right away, and we often only want to do things we're "good" at. We put so much pressure on ourselves that we lose the joy and wonder that come from being a beginner.

To free ourselves from this mentality, we need to give ourselves permission to experiment. The purpose of experiments is to try things out and gather data about how it goes. We can then reevaluate as we move along. Again, we don't have to commit to something forever. We can always change our minds and shift gears, and experimenting with different ways of doing things helps nurture our flexibility. In some situations, the stakes feel much lower when we're just "seeing what happens." This is a less risky-feeling way to dabble in uncertainty. Using this language of "experiment" gives us courage and helps us not take our endeavors (or ourselves!) too seriously.

You have full permission to start small. Experimenting with a new workout class or new recipe might feel inconsequential, but it's not! Even with lower-stakes experiments, you're learning and growing by challenging your unhelpful beliefs and putting yourself out in the world. Most of us arrived at self-abandonment through a proverbial "death by a thousand cuts," so it makes sense if you need to make lots of small changes to get to a very different place in the future. Don't start with an experiment that will blow up your life, like leaving your family or haphazardly quitting your job and moving across the country. Start small and build from there.

Your experiments won't always go well. You might have to walk out of that hot yoga class after ten minutes because you're about to pass out. The new recipe might be disgusting and everyone ends up eating cereal instead. Maybe you'll try three therapists before you find the one you click with, or maybe during your trial separation, you realize you really do miss your partner and aren't at all interested in getting a divorce. The goal is not to "get it right" on the first try. Rather, it's to be open to showing up and trying something new and simply seeing what happens.

No matter the outcome, don't beat up on yourself afterward. Instead, lean into nonjudgment, curiosity, and compassion.

Permission to Be Human

We expect ourselves to be superhumans. We're conditioned to believe we should be perfect, do it all, and never run out of energy or have a hair out of place. In many ways, we want ourselves to be machines: *I know I've been tired, but I slept for a solid eight hours last night, so I should be back in business running at full capacity today.* We dislike our inherent messiness. Our humanness.

We hereby grant you permission to be human. You're allowed to make mistakes, get things wrong, make bad choices, lose your temper, have a meltdown, not have it all together, drop the ball, forget, whine, complain, half-ass it, accidentally pass gas in public, put your foot in your mouth, or wear the "wrong" thing. All these things can happen. It doesn't make you a bad person. It doesn't make you flawed. It only makes you human.

From the little ways we're human, like forgetting to bring snacks to the first grade soccer game, to the big ways we're human, like forgetting to turn off the camera when we take a bathroom break during a Zoom meeting, let's trade judgment and shame for grace and compassion. Can our mistakes just be something we did rather than meaning something about who we are?

To get there, you'll need to use all the skills you've learned thus far: taking responsibility, making repairs, being vulnerable, speaking truth, and so on. Instead of thinking, *I'm a horrible person who totally messed up*, try telling yourself, *I'm so human* or *That was such a human moment.* The latter phrasing allows you to soften into connecting with and truly supporting yourself.

For some reason, we imagine that other people will like us less if we're human. But actually, people like us more when we show our humanity. As we talked about in the section on vulnerability in chapter five, we like *real* people. *Human* people. We don't love our friends and family *despite* their messy and human pieces, we love them *because* of their messy humanness.

Permission to Rest

For many women, this is the permission we need to give ourselves the most: the permission to stop and to rest. We've been trained to go, go, go and be busy, busy, busy and to do it all fast and furiously. This conditioning makes it so that we simply don't have much time and space available for rest.

But there's a second, perhaps more important, layer here. Even if we *do* have free time and space, many women have a hard time actually *resting*. Does this sound familiar? We feel guilty for being still, for not being productive, and for "wasting" time. Since we're ambivalent about giving ourselves permission to rest, we end up in what we call the "purgatory of rest." This occurs when we aren't engaged in something productive, but neither are we actually relaxing. Rest purgatory might take the form of mindlessly scrolling on our devices or trying to relax in a bubble bath while our minds are racing with all the things we "should" be doing. Neither is very restorative.

Here is your permission slip to rest. Make yourself a visible permission slip, whether it's putting a simple sticky note on your bathroom mirror that reminds you to take ten minutes to rest, scheduling a rest appointment on your calendar, or creating a phone display background that says, "You're allowed to rest." Give yourself permission to intentionally *do* less so you can *be* more.

Permission to Be Flexible

Flexibility can be hard! How do you respond when your flight is delayed or canceled? What about when you show up to your favorite restaurant only to find it's closed for a private event? Or when you try to log on for a big work presentation to discover your computer isn't working? Do you roll with the punches, or are you more likely to become irritable, flustered, and overwhelmed when plans unexpectedly change?

Flexibility is especially difficult for those of us who are more "Type A" and wired with tendencies toward rigidity and control. We have a hard time pivoting and changing course when life doesn't go according to plan. While inflexibility is a strategy to increase our sense of control, it actually leads to more stress and anxiety. When has your life ever actually gone to plan, exactly as you laid it out, all day, every day?

The more rigid and inflexible we are, the more stress and anxiety we feel. Life is full of uncontrollable, uncertain things. This can become a never-ending feedback loop: Rigid controlling leads to more stress and anxiety, which leads to more rigid controlling, which increases stress and anxiety, and on and on. Being flexible allows us to focus on the things we can actually control, which in turn, lessens our stress and anxiety.

Flexibility allows us to continually tune back into our IGS. When life throws us a curveball, instead of resisting, melting down, or having a mini panic attack, we can notice any discomfort and distress, make space for it to belong, practice accepting what is, and then respond according to our values and what matters most to us. For instance, let's say you have a casserole cooking in the oven when a college friend texts you that they have a layover and want to meet up for drinks. In this situation, do you ditch the casserole (and any associated guilt) to meet up with them, or do you stick with your dinner plans? Practicing flexibility frees you up to check in and change your course rather than letting external forces or internal rules make that decision for you. Flexibility allows you to adapt your thinking as well as your actions, and when you harness flexibility, you tend to feel calmer, more centered and present, and at peace.

Do Try This at Home

#1: Upgrade Your Thinking

Upgrading your thinking takes time and practice. Here are some helpful reminders as you figure out what works for you. Feel free to take a snapshot to use as the background on your phone, or write some of these with a dry-erase marker on your bathroom mirror.

- I have permission to drop expectations, comparisons, perfectionistic standards, and unhelpful stories.
- I have permission to offer myself more acceptance and flexibility.
- I have permission to change my mind, experiment, and rest.
- I have permission to be human and flexible.
- I have permission to stay connected to myself and show up in the world with authenticity and vulnerability.

#2: Create Your Own Permission Slip

What else do you need permission for? To take a break from the gym? To be honest about how you're feeling or what you want and need? To not check your email after 6 p.m.? To play video games?

We give you permission to create your own permission slips. Think big here. What's limiting you, and what sort of permission would free you up? What sort of permission would create more peace and ease in your life? Write yourself that permission slip now.

#3: Take Things Off Your To-Do List

Pick one to three items you can take off your to-do list, or create a *not*-to-do list. Maybe these items won't get done at all, or maybe you'll ask for help and outsource them. Or maybe press the easy button every now and then and give yourself the break you deserve.

Conclusion:
The Essential You

When we were brand new psychologists, we believed we could help people get rid of feelings of not-enoughness. This was often one of the expressed goals in therapy: to build self-esteem and finally feel "enough." We've learned over the years that this is an impossible task. Our feelings of not-enoughness are part of being human, especially for women. We're not going to get rid of these feelings, and our efforts to outrun them ultimately end in self-abandonment. However, we can learn to work *with* these feelings and relate to them with kindness and compassion.

Whether you initially picked up this book because you were tired of being exhausted, stuck, irritable, "blah," or uninspired, deep down you've probably known for a while that you were ready for change. That nudge from deep down was the first whisper from your IGS coming back online and inviting you to rediscover the lost pieces of you.

So, what have you heard her say as you've read this book? What are your next steps?

We hope you've learned to welcome discomfort, make space for not-enoughness, and allow self-trust to grow. Remember, there's room for *all* of it. The more we take up space in our own lives, the more connected we become with ourselves and others. Regardless of where you are in this journey, you should feel proud.

In fact, this calls for a celebration!

How can you celebrate the return of your muchness? How can you throw yourself a "welcome home" party?

Essential Truths

As you go out into the world and continue to create a life well lived, it's only natural that self-abandonment will resurface from time to time. When it does, we invite you to keep coming back to these essential truths. Think of them as a compass that will lead you back to *you*.

You Are the Expert in You

Trust yourself. Keep coming back to your own wisdom and intuition. Reconnect with your IGS over and over and over again. No one can give you the answer to who you are and the path you should follow; you get to discover this for yourself. The world is going to pressure you to focus outward, to look outside yourself to an EGS for answers and validation. You cannot stay connected to yourself or others if you are moving too fast or doing too much. Instead, slow down and stay connected to your IGS. She's always there for you, and she won't let you down.

You Are Already Enough, Just as You Are

Beginning with our own personal stories in the introduction, not-enoughness has come up time and time again throughout this book. It fuels diet culture, capitalism, uber-productivity, and our own quests for self-improvement. Not-enoughness gets us caught in self-judgment, comparisons, and perfectionism and makes vulnerability feel scary and even impossible at times. Notice your judgments. They do nothing but make you feel bad. Become an expert at catching and interrupting your judgments. Reach for curiosity and compassion instead, which have a magical way of slicing through and softening our judgments and harsh criticisms. Put simply, we feel more peaceful and settled when we choose compassion and curiosity over judgment.

Not-enoughness underlies all forms of self-abandonment, and, yes, you will have *feelings* of not-enoughness pop in from time to time. This does not mean that *you* are not enough. Not-enoughness is a feeling just like all the others we have and is a normal part of being human. Instead of getting swept away in your feelings of not-enoughness, make friends with those feelings. Have compassion and let it all belong.

Discomfort Is Unavoidable, and You Can Handle It

There is no such thing as a pain-free life. Discomfort is inherently unavoidable and our efforts to go around or hide from discomfort typically result in *more* discomfort.

So, if discomfort is a normal and natural part of the package of being human, how can you learn to tolerate it well? Instead of running from it, fighting with it, or numbing it in some way, make friends with your discomfort. Make space for discomfort and lean into it with gentleness, curiosity, and compassion. Practice self-soothing and reaching for support. Like all feelings, discomfort is temporary, like waves on a beach.

Practice telling yourself, *Yes, this is uncomfortable, and it feels hard. But I've got this.* Bonus points if you literally stand tall, with your chest held high and your arms open, while saying this to yourself.

Speak Truth

We often avoid honesty to avoid discomfort, but truth-telling is where we have to start. We must listen to ourselves and then speak our truth. As women, we are constantly reinforced for being nice, polite, and agreeable. But true belonging and authentic connection with others *require* us to tell the truth. So, blaze your own truth-telling trails. Using your voice to communicate your truth to the world is an act of rebellion against all the societal structures built to keep you silent.

Start small. Have patience with yourself and keep at it. Allow yourself to get out of the habit of saying yes automatically. Practice setting healthy boundaries and saying no to create space in your life for you.

Be Intentional

Greg McKeown, author of *Essentialism: The Disciplined Pursuit of Less*, writes, "If you don't prioritize your life, someone else will" (p. 10).[62] Take some time to think about what that quote is saying.

It's time for you to get in the driver's seat of your life. As we've discussed, self-abandonment often happens little by little over time, like a death by a thousand cuts. Staying connected to yourself requires you to make ongoing conscious decisions about what is most essential to you. You must continually make intentional choices about how you want to show up in your life.

When you tune in, ask yourself what matters most to you. List the priorities you would like to place above all others.

Yes, there will be consequences. Prioritizing one goal might mean sacrificing another, and that is okay. Not everything can be essential. We often have to say no to clear space for us to say yes to our top priority.

Choose Abundance Over Scarcity

Play, fun, joy, and wonder are not optional life experiences; they make life worth living. Every time you prioritize these essential things in your life, you stay true to yourself.

If you want to live a life of meaning and richness, you must start tapping into pleasure and desire, fun and play, joy and wonder. An abundance mindset means knowing there is enough joy to go around; connection and love are not finite resources. But a scarcity mindset tells you there is not enough of anything. A scarcity mindset makes you think *you* are not enough, leaving you feeling burned out and disconnected from yourself and the people around you.

Whereas a scarcity mindset brings feelings of constriction and exhaustion, an abundance mindset feels more open and freeing, more spacious and gracious. You have a choice. You have permission to choose abundance.

As we close our time together, we invite you to tune inward once more. Imagine your IGS as a younger version of you. Take a moment and really picture this younger version of yourself.

Can you see her skipping up to your front door? She's joyful, unafraid, brave, and playful. Without any hesitation, she knocks on your door and beckons you to come outside. "I've missed you!" she says. "I know it's been a long time since we've been together, but I'm so glad you're here."

Appendix: Feelings List

Unpleasant, Unwanted, Uncomfortable Feelings

Sad	Afraid	Angry
Down Depressed Hopeless Helpless Rejected Miserable Hurt Discouraged Disappointed	Worried Anxious Tense Restless Nervous On edge Panicky Frightened Terrified	Hostile Frustrated Irritable Agitated Bitter Outraged Mad Livid Furious Spiteful Annoyed
Dead Ass Last	**Not Enough**	**Other Hard Feelings**
Overwhelmed Exhausted Weary Tired Depleted Fatigued Burned out Listless Lifeless Sluggish Unmotivated Resentful	Insecure Embarrassed Ashamed Incompetent Worthless Insignificant Invisible Weak Inferior Unseen Pitiful	Guilty Envious Jealous Bored Shy Bashful Confused Disgusted Lonely Regretful Betrayed

Pleasant, Wanted, Desirable Feelings

Happy	**Chill**	**Capable**
Content Joyful Thrilled Delighted Glad Cheerful Vibrant Tickled	Relaxed Calm Peaceful Soothed Gentle Flexible Accepting Rested	Proud Competent Accomplished Confident Strong Brave Fierce Courageous
Energized	**Engaged**	**Connected**
Motivated Excited Lively Adventurous Enthusiastic Inspired Hopeful Stimulated Eager	Appreciative Grateful Awed Surprised Interested Curious Amused Engrossed Enchanted Fascinated	Safe Loved Secure Close Warm Tender Friendly Affectionate Sympathetic Empathetic Compassionate Cooperative

Endnotes

1 Burton, T. (Director). (2010). *Alice in wonderland* [Film]. Walt Disney Pictures.

2 Hall, E. (2024). "I have been a thousand different women." In *Made of rivers* (p. 54). Hay House.

3 Braun, R. (2023, November 15). *Five reasons your self-care isn't working and how to change it.* Forbes. https://www.forbes.com/sites/forbescoachescouncil/2023/11/15/five-reasons-your-self-care-isnt-working-and-how-to-change-it

4 Chojnacki, R. (2024, June 20). *The great escape: Exploring the rise of the joy economy.* Circana. https://www.circana.com/post/the-great-escape-exploring-the-rise-of-the-joy-economy

5 Ghlionn, J. M. (2024, June 27). *Taylor Swift is not a good role model.* Newsweek. https://www.newsweek.com/taylor-swift-not-good-role-model-opinion-1916799

6 Christler, J. C. (2008). 2007 Presidential Address: Fear of losing control: Power, perfectionism, and the psychology of women. *Psychology of Women Quarterly, 32*, 1–12. https://doi.org/10.1111/j.1471-6402.2007.00402.x

7 Johnson, A. G. (2005). *The gender knot: Unraveling our patriarchal legacy* (2nd ed.). Temple University Press.

8 Higgins, C. (2018, June 22). *The age of patriarchy: How an unfashionable idea became a rallying cry for feminism today.* The Guardian. https://www.theguardian.com/news/2018/jun/22/the-age-of-patriarchy-how-an-unfashionable-idea-became-a-rallying-cry-for-feminism-today

9 Bianchi, S. M., Milkie, M. A., Sayer, L. C., & Robinson, J. P. (2000). Is anyone doing the housework? Trends in the gender division of household labor. *Social Forces, 79*(1), 191–228. https://doi.org/10.2307/2675569

10 Coltrane, S. (2000). Research on household labor: Modeling and measuring the social embeddedness of routine family work. *Journal of Marriage and Family, 62*(4), 1208–1233. https://doi.org/10.1111/j.1741-3737.2000.01208.x

11 Suddath, C. (2024, March 28). *What do we owe women for child care and housework? $3.6 trillion.* Bloomberg. https://www.bloomberg.com/news/newsletters/2024-03-28/what-do-we-owe-women-for-child-care-and-housework-3-6-trillion

12 Rodsky, E. (2019). *Fair play: A game-changing solution for when you have too much to do (and more life to live).* G. P. Putnam's Sons.

13 Schaeffer, K. (2024, February 27). *For Women's History Month, a look at gender gains—and gaps—in the US.* PEW Research Center. https://www.pewresearch.org/short-reads/2024/02/27/for-womens-history-month-a-look-at-gender-gains-and-gaps-in-the-us

14 Witter, A. (2024, January 9). *9 facts you need to know about gender inequality.* One. https://www.one.org/stories/facts-gender-equality

15 Lankford, K. (2023, April 28). *Pink tax: What does price discrimination cost women?* U.S. News. https://money.usnews.com/money/personal-finance/taxes/articles/the-pink-tax-costs-women-thousands-of-dollars-over-their-lifetimes

16 Schaeffer, K. (2024, February 27). *For Women's History Month, a look at gender gains—and gaps—in the US.* PEW Research Center. https://www.pewresearch.org/short-reads/2024/02/27/for-womens-history-month-a-look-at-gender-gains-and-gaps-in-the-us

17 Allamano, C. B. (2020, November 27). *Paid paternity leave should be the norm in the US.* World Economic Forum. https://www.weforum.org/agenda/2020/11/paid-paternity-leave-in-the-united-states

18 Schaeffer, K. (2024, February 27). *For Women's History Month, a look at gender gains—and gaps—in the US.* PEW Research Center. https://www.pewresearch.org/short-reads/2024/02/27/for-womens-history-month-a-look-at-gender-gains-and-gaps-in-the-us

19 Olya, G. (2022, March 7). *Women pay $8k more than men during length of car ownership—let's change that.* Yahoo Finance. https://finance.yahoo.com/news/women-pay-8k-more-men-190001588.html?

20 Michon, K. (2024, August 29). *Women buying cars.* NOLO. https://www.nolo.com/legal-encyclopedia/women-buying-cars-30335.html

21 Katz Institute for Women's Health. (n.d.). *Gaslighting in women's health: No, it's not just in your head.* Northwell Health. https://www.northwell.edu/katz-institute-for-womens-health/articles/gaslighting-in-womens-health

22 Shoenthal, A. (2024, January 12). *Despite increased awareness, gender bias persists across healthcare.* Forbes. https://www.forbes.com/sites/amyshoenthal/2024/01/12/despite-increased-awareness-gender-bias-persists-across-healthcare

23 Anyangwe, E., & Mahtani, M. (2023, August 3). *What is patriarchy? What does it mean and why is everyone talking about it?* CNN. https://www.cnn.com/2023/08/03/world/what-is-patriarchy-explainer-as-equals-intl-cmd/index.html

24 Tagle, A., & Schneider, C. M. (2022, January 4). *Diet culture is everywhere. Here's how to fight it.* NPR. https://www.npr.org/2021/12/23/1067210075/what-if-the-best-diet-is-to-reject-diet-culture

25 Marshall, M. (Ed.). (2022, April 4). *Diet & weight loss.* Harvard Health Publishing. https://www.health.harvard.edu/topics/diet-and-weight-loss

26 Chastain, R. (2021, November 6). *Who says dieting fails most of the time?* Weight and Healthcare. https://weightandhealthcare.substack.com/p/who-says-dieting-fails-the-majority

27 Petruzzi, D. (2024, November 14). *Value of the global anti-aging products market 2022–2032.* Statistica. https://www.statista.com/statistics/509679/value-of-the-global-anti-aging-market

28 Diehl, A., Dzubinski, L. M., & Stephenson, A. L. (2023, June 16). *Women in leadership face ageism at every age.* Harvard Business Review. https://hbr.org/2023/06/women-in-leadership-face-ageism-at-every-age

29 Kasser, T. (2002). *The high price of materialism.* Bradford Books.

30 Neff, K. (2021). *Fierce self-compassion: How women can harness kindness to speak up, claim their power, and thrive.* Harper.

31 Neff, K. D. (2023). Self-compassion: Theory, method, research, and intervention. *Annual Review of Psychology, 74*, 193–218. https://doi.org/10.1146/annurev-psych-032420-031047

32 Neff, K. (2011). *Self-compassion: The proven power of being kind to yourself.* William Morrow Paperbacks.

33 Bauer, J. J., Graham, L. E., Lauber, E. A., & Lynch, B. P. (2019). What growth sounds like: Redemption, self-improvement, and eudaimonic growth across different life narratives in relation to well-being. *Journal of Personality, 87*(3), 546–565. https://doi.org/10.1111/jopy.12414

34 Veilleux, J. C., Clift, J. B., Brott, K. H., Warner, E. A., Schreiber, R. E., Henderson, H. M., & Shelton, D. K. (2024). "I'm so dumb and worthless *right now*": Factors associated with heightened momentary self-criticism in daily life. *Cognition and Emotion, 38*(4), 1–16. https://doi.org/10.1080/02699931.2024.2305400

35 May, G. G. (2009). *Will and spirit.* HarperCollins Publishers.

36 Leotti, L. A., Iyengar, S. S., & Ochsner, K. N. (2010). Born to choose: The origins and value of the need for control. *Trends in Cognitive Sciences, 14*(10), 457–463. https://doi.org/10.1016/j.tics.2010.08.001

37 Moss-Racusin, C. A., & Rudman, L. A. (2010). Disruptions in women's self-promotion: The backlash avoidance model. *Psychology of Women Quarterly, 34*(2), 186–202. https://doi.org/10.1111/j.1471-6402.2010.01561.x

38 Exley, C. L., & Kessler, J. B. (2022). The gender gap in self-promotion. *The Quarterly Journal of Economics, 137*(3), 1345–1381. https://doi.org/10.1093/qje/qjac003

39 Loehnen, E. (2023). *On our best behavior: The seven deadly sins and the price women pay to be good.* The Dial Press.

40 Gross, J. J. (2002). Emotion regulation: Affective, cognitive, and social consequences. *Psychophysiology, 39*(3), 281–291. https://doi.org/10.1017/S0048577201393198

41 Aldao, A., & Nolen-Hoeksema, S. (2010). Specificity of cognitive emotion regulation strategies: A transdiagnostic examination. *Behaviour Research and Therapy, 48*(10), 974–983. https://doi.org/10.1016/j.brat.2010.06.002

42 Aldao, A., Nolen-Hoeksema, S., & Schweizer, S. (2010). Emotion-regulation strategies across psychopathology: A meta-analytic review. *Clinical Psychology Review, 30*(2), 217–237. https://doi.org/10.1016/j.cpr.2009.11.004

43 Wakelin, K. E., Perman, G., & Simonds, L. M. (2021). Effectiveness of self-compassion-related interventions for reducing self-criticism: A systematic review and meta-analysis. *Clinical Psychology and Psychotherapy, 29*(1), 1–25. https://doi.org/10.1002/cpp.2586

44 Baumeister, R. F., & Leary, M. R. (1995). The need to belong: Desire for interpersonal attachments as a fundamental human motivation. *Psychological Bulletin, 117*(3), 497–529. https://doi.org/10.1037/0033-2909.117.3.497

45 Eisenberger, N. I., Lieberman, M. D., & Williams, K. D. (2003). Does rejection hurt? An fMRI study of social exclusion. *Science, 302*(5643), 290–292. https://doi.org/10.1126/science.1089134

46 Brinke, L., Lee, J., & Carney, D. (2015). The physiology of (dis)honesty: Does it impact health? *Current Opinion in Psychology, 6*, 177–182. https://doi.org/10.1016/j.copsyc.2015.08.004

47 Brown, B. (2018). *Dare to lead: Brave work. Tough conversations. Whole hearts.* Random House.

48 Brown, B. (2012). *Daring greatly: How the courage to be vulnerable transforms the way we live, love, parent, and lead.* Avery.

49 Hall, K. D., & Cook, M. H. (2011). *The power of validation: Arming your child against bullying, peer pressure, addiction, self-harm, and out-of-control emotions.* New Harbinger Publications.

50 Drescher, A. (2024, January 23). *Codependency: Are you caretaking or caregiving?* SimplyPsychology. https://www.simplypsychology.org/caretaking-vs-caregiving.html

51 Chamorro-Premuzic, T. (2013, August 22). *Why do so many incompetent men become leaders?* Harvard Business Review. https://hbr.org/2013/08/why-do-so-many-incompetent-men

52 Hertz, N. (2010, November). *How to use experts and when not to* [Video]. TED Conferences. https://www.ted.com/talks/noreena_hertz_how_to_use_experts_and_when_not_to

53 Gupta, S. (2024, January 8). *What is the blame game?* Verywell Mind. https://www.verywellmind.com/blame-game-definition-signs-impact-and-prevention-5215208

54 Cooks-Campbell, A. (2021, December 10). *Victim mentality: How we hold ourselves back by blaming others.* BetterUp. https://www.betterup.com/blog/victim-mentality

55 Raypole, C. (2023, March 15). *How to identify and deal with a victim mentality.* Healthline. https://www.healthline.com/health/victim-mentality

56 Amaryah, A. (2023, July 7). *How to tell if your desire to be self-sufficient is actually toxic hyper-independence—and what to do about it.* Well+Good. https://www.wellandgood.com/hyper-independence

57 Cherry, K. (2025, January 27). *The basics of prosocial behavior.* Verywell mind. https://www.verywellmind.com/what-is-prosocial-behavior-2795479

58 Raposa, E. B., Laws, H.B., and Ansell, E. B. (2016). Prosocial behavior mitigates the negative effects of stress in everyday life. *Clinical Psychological Science, 4*(4), 691–698. https://doi.org/10.1177/2167702615611073

59 Neff, K. (2021). *Fierce self-compassion: How women can harness kindness to speak up, claim their power, and thrive.* Harper.

60 Kennedy, B. (2022). *Good inside: A guide to becoming the parent you want to be.* Harper Wave.

61 van Putten, M., Zeelenberg, M., & van Dijk, E. (2010). Who throws good money after bad? Action vs. state orientation moderates the sunk cost fallacy. *Judgment and Decision Making, 5*(1), 33–36. https://doi.org/10.1017/S1930297500002011

62 McKeown, G. (2014). *Essentialism: The disciplined pursuit of less.* Crown Business.

Acknowledgments

From Avery

To the family I was born into and the one I got to choose, I simply would not be the person I am without each of you. I am blessed beyond measure by your presence in my life.

To John, for being my lighthouse in the storm. You have held my hand on the best and worst days of my life. Your encouragement gives me confidence to be my authentic self every day. I am so lucky to be married to you and I love the life we've built together.

To Wes, for your patience, unending enthusiasm, and sincere interest in my work. Your creativity and brilliance inspire me and fill me with pride. I love you, and I love being your mom.

To Sam, Kathy, Parke, and Ellie, and to my extended family of grandparents, aunts, uncles, and cousins, who have surrounded me with unconditional love and support my entire life. I cherish each of you. Your wisdom, compassion, and belief in me have motivated me to do more than I ever thought was possible.

To my nieces and nephews, for being the siblings Wes never had and for giving your time and affection so generously to me and my family. Being your aunt is an honor and a privilege (and so much fun!).

To my in-laws and outlaws, for your love and acceptance. I treasure my relationships with each of you more than you will ever know.

To Kirsten, for comforting me in times of grief, cheering me on in times of celebration, and making me laugh throughout it all—together, we're unlimited.

To Erica, for your faith and friendship. From playdates when our kids were tiny to happy hours and girls' trips, you have brought so much balance and joy into my life.

To Chris and Elida, for loving me and my family as your own.

To Jamie and Lucy, for being the most amazing friends, colleagues, and coauthors in the world, and to Taylor, for bringing us back to ourselves.

From Lucy

First and foremost, thank you to Avery and Jamie for being such badass colleagues and friends. Talk about authentic, real, true selves! Our creative endeavors—this book, the podcast, branding and rebranding, retreats, coaching, workshops, our new office space—have added zest and vibrancy to my life, paving the way for a more multidimensional and fulfilling future. You're so easy to work with and so fun to spend time with, and somehow our collective effort shifts potential overwhelm and drudgery to ease and excitement. What a gift that we align so well!

To my dear friend Natalie, where do I even begin? I trace this wild journey of reconnection and reclamation back to you—to your invitation to join you for a crazy retreat in Maine. You're one of the most amazing humans I know, and it's been a joy and a balm to my soul to do this work alongside you. I treasure our friendship, and I miss you all the time. Can we create a portal between Niwot and Dallas?

To Taylor, you were right. Retreats really are your superpower. I truly would be lost without you. Thank you for helping me thaw and unstick from my relentless thinking. I wasn't sure such peace and ease were possible for my adult self. Thank you for reminding me to show up fully human, even as messy and uncomfortable as that might feel at times. It's totally worth it.

Lastly, to my amazing family, I love each and every one of you so much (dare I say I love you the most?). Thank you for caring both *about* and *for* me. Thank you for being so stable and consistent, ever present and dependable. I often feel I won the jackpot in terms of families. I could not ask for more.

Addison and Charlotte, it has been an honor and privilege to be your mom. You are fierce, and you are so incredibly precious. I never want you to abandon yourselves! You— the essence of who you are, the pieces that make you unique, all the imperfections and all the strengths—are absolutely enough, just as you are. The world needs your light, which shines brightest when you allow all the parts of you to belong. Thank you for reminding me of the importance of staying connected to myself, mostly so I could be connected to you.

And last but not least, to Brent, as you're fond of saying, "Teamwork makes the dream work," and I can think of no one I'd rather have on my closest team than you. Thank you for your ceaseless encouragement. From offering a listening ear to asking good questions to picking up the slack at home to cheerleading progress (or lack thereof), your unwavering support means the world to me. Thank you for the permission to take time for myself and permission to run wild with all these plans and projects. I love you.

From Jamie

Thank you to my husband and the love of my life, Robert. You have always supported me, especially when I have doubted myself. You've helped bring down my walls, taught me to be humble and generous, and showed me the importance of giving people second chances.

To my kiddos, Grace and Max. Grace, you once were my feisty, two-pound, twelve-ounce newborn, and now you're my super cool, unique, rockin' high-schooler-cat-lady with the biggest heart. I love that you've found your voice at such a young age and aren't afraid to speak the truth. You inspire me to have hard conversations and to be honest even when I'm afraid. I love you dearly, and you will always be my Lulu. Max, you are the personification of joy. I've never met someone who's so quick to smile and is filled to the brim with excitement and positivity. Your good-natured heart and quickness to forgive are constant reminders that I need to give others the benefit of the doubt. You make me laugh and help me not take life too seriously. I love you, buddy.

To my little sister, Hillary. You are my absolute favorite person, full stop. You have the best sense of humor and inspire me to be creative and try new things. I now have a serious gardening addiction because of you, and lord only knows how much money the Disney company has gotten from me because of our mutual "hobby." You help me find my "muchness" every day.

To my closest and dearest friends, Sarah and Megan, I love you both. Your unwavering support and encouragement have meant the world to me. You've each taught me that it's okay to be a vulnerable, unfiltered, and messy human, and I'm forever grateful.

Thank you to Taylor, for your guidance and wisdom and for being an example of loving and compassionate leadership that this world so desperately needs.

To my dear friends, coauthors, and badass humans, Avery and Lucy. Thank you both for embarking on this crazy book-writing journey with me. You push me in the best possible ways while giving me permission to slow down when I need it. I am stronger knowing you are both on my side.

About the Authors

DR. AVERY HOENIG received a PhD in clinical psychology from the University of Texas Southwestern Medical Center in 2004. In her private practice, she uses cognitive behavioral therapy (CBT) to help older adolescents and adults manage symptoms of anxiety and depression. Avery is happiest when she's watching live music, telling stories around a campfire, or holding baby animals.

DR. LUCY SMITH received a PhD in clinical psychology from the University of Colorado at Boulder in 2008. She works in private practice, specializing in the treatment of eating disorders. Lucy enjoys a good night's sleep in fresh sheets, spending time in the mountains, and reading on her kindle (especially young adult fantasy fiction!).

DR. JAMIE WILSON received a PhD in counseling psychology from the University of North Texas in 2011. In her private practice, Jamie specializes in the treatment of anxiety, trauma, and relationship difficulties. In her spare time, she can be found meticulously planning her next Disney escape, like the fairy godmother she is, or prancing around her garden whispering sweet nothings to her peonies.

In addition to their private practices, Avery, Lucy, and Jamie host a fun and informative podcast, *Inspiration from the Couch*, which covers a wide array of mental health topics. They founded *The Badass Rebellion*, a movement to help extraordinary women stop being everything but themselves.